My Journey Trusting the Lord

PASTOR MICHAEL STAAB

ISBN 979-8-89243-131-6 (paperback)
ISBN 979-8-89243-132-3 (digital)

Christian Faith Publishing
832 Park Avenue
Meadville, PA 16335
www.christianfaithpublishing.com

Printed in the United States of America

CONTENTS

PREFACE

This book is about a man's encounter with God, his relationship with Him, and his love for Him. It's about the trials and tribulations that God led the man and his family through. It's about business and relationship trials, trusting God through those trials, and trusting Him for what is about to come.

INTRODUCTION

Throughout my life, the most important thing I have learned is to trust the Lord. I have encountered countless trials and tribulations, from money problems to deaths. Through it all, trusting the Lord has brought me through all of them. Because I trusted in the Lord, I have been able to help others learn to do the same. This book tells my story, which is a story of the Lord's love. I tell stories about my childhood, my marriages, my children, and my journey with the Lord. I hope that I can inspire you to trust the Lord with all of your heart because He will never let you down.

1

SALVATION

It's the beginning of Lent in 1975. My name is Michael Staab; I am twenty-one years old and own a heating and air-conditioning company named Jerome L. Staab & Sons Inc. in Pittsburgh, Pennsylvania, with my three brothers—Gerald, Dave, and Tom. The company was given to us in 1974 by my father, Jerome L. Staab who started it in 1929. It was a Wednesday afternoon- almost quitting time- and I was talking with one of our employees named Michael K. He was a Christian and was a year or two younger than me. He was hired by my brother, Dave, and had been learning the trade with us for a couple of years. His work practices impressed me. I used to drive him home from work in my Z28 1968 Camaro, and we would talk. There was a buzz among my brothers and the other workers as they would test his Christianity by laying Playboy magazines on his seat in the truck to see what he would do with them.

When Michael K. got into the truck, he would simply toss them aside. At 4:00 p.m., a half hour before quitting time, my brothers, the other workers, and I would gather at the refrigerator and have ourselves a beer or two. Mike K. would keep working, making ductwork for the next job right until 4:30 p.m., quitting time. Then he would come down and I would ride him home. He was always prompt in getting to work in the morning as well. I did not realize it at the time, but this was when God was reeling me in. Mike K. was honest and followed the rules.

In our conversation, I told Mike K. that I was planning a trip to California to see what the girls were like there even though I was dating my high school sweetheart, Audrey. Mike K. began to question me about my motives for such a trip and invited me to a prayer meeting called Light of the Cross hosted by a man named Tommy M. They held the meetings on Wednesday nights in a community center hall located on Bower Hill Road in the Upper Saint Clair/Scott Township Area, a suburb of Pittsburgh, and I decided to check it out. I don't know what made me go. I thought I was having a pretty good time otherwise. I used to drink a lot, puff a little marijuana from time to time, race cars, chase girls, and get into fights when I had to with my buddies. I lived in Arlington, a rough neighborhood in Pittsburgh, and hung out with three groups of friends.

One group was the fighters and the roughnecks. The second group was the sports group as I loved to play basketball, football, etc. The last group was a group from my neighborhood in a different section of the city called Beechview. I could write another book on all of the things we did as juveniles. But now I was a man, owning a company with my brothers. I was at the end of my second year of college at Robert Morris studying business administration, and here I was riding my Z28 Camaro to a prayer meeting.

On my way there, I began to remember my other friends in high school who were drug addicts-turned-Christians. I remember them telling me about this experience they had with God called being "born again," but I kind of brushed it off. I thought it was good for them and I was glad they believed in God. It wasn't that I didn't believe, but not like they did. They were different than they used to be and completely stopped doing drugs. I also remember when I was an altar boy and served mass for Father Bench in my sixth through eighth grades. I remember telling my parents in eighth grade that I wanted to be a priest. I also remember the Franciscan sisters who taught me at Saint Henry's and the sound of my father singing "How Great Thou Art" when we would go to church. But all of that changed in high school. My focus turned to girls, sex, alcohol, friends, parties, etc. Now high school was over, and all of that stuff dwindled. My longtime girlfriend, Audrey, was getting restless as to our next step after five years of dating. I guess things were all coming to a head. Then I walked through the door of the prayer meeting.

It was a hall, but the holy fervor I felt took me back to when I served mass with Father Bench in the eighth grade. The message that night, regarding premarital sex, seemed to be aimed at me; I loved it and could not imagine that He only blesses sex in the marriage bed (yes, you have to be married). I left the meeting intrigued and began to ponder this sex thing. Mike K. encouraged me to come back to another meeting. Each time I came back, the message reflected another spotlight on my life and how I was treating other people. I began to search the Bible to see if premarital sex was acceptable but was convicted at every turn. It was during this time that my girlfriend, Audrey, began to notice I was kinder to her. She became interested in these prayer meetings as she believed they had a positive effect on me.

One night, Audrey and two of our friends, Russ and Dee, decided to come with us to the prayer meeting. The prayer meeting started, and suddenly, there was a disruption. A man in the audience stood up and was making comments about a plane trip and how the airline people carried him off the plane; none of it made sense. So the prayer group leader, Tommy M., asked him to sit down. The meeting was brought back into order and continued. And then it happened…

Tommy M. asked anyone who wished to ask the Lord Jesus Christ into their hearts and forgive them of their sins to please raise their hands. All four of us raised our hands. I did not realize it at the time or know exactly what I was feeling, but it was a strong sense of that fervor I used to feel serving mass with Father Bench; it was a strong holiness. We were all asked to come forward, which we did, and then asked the Lord Jesus Christ into our hearts and to forgive us for our sins. I remember feeling great peace, joy, and love fall upon me and enter into my heart; I was astonished. God was real and how wonderful it was. The eyes of our understanding were opened; God was real and alive with his peace, joy, and love living inside my heart. When the meeting ended, all four of us had come to Christ. We had such excitement. Truly nothing like this had ever happened to us before. I remember seeing Michael K. and the first thing that came to my mind as I laid eyes upon him was that now I had it, too. I realized now it was Christ that drew me to him. Now I had Christ too.

The four of us left the prayer meeting after fellowshipping like four drunken sailors. We were riding home in my Z28 Camaro, but now this was very different. We all had this great freedom, filled with the love of God, great joy, and peace. We were like drunkards, carrying on in a good way, but without alcohol or weed. Our lives were now changed. We were like what happened to the Apostles when they broke out of the upper room and the people of Jerusalem said they were like drunkards. I look back and also see how the devil tried to block us all that night when the man stood up and tried to take over the prayer meeting.

Thank God for Tommy M. who brought it under subjection and brought the prayer meeting into order so that we could all find Christ and thank God for Michael K. for being the witness that drew me to Christ. I am forever grateful to these Christians who were obedient and took the time to reach out to the sinners like us. I look back and realize we were lost, but he loved us first before we ever knew him. He died for us and saved us when we did not even realize that we needed to be saved. He sent these people into our lives, drew us to Himself, and saved us. I realized that I was truly searching for someone or something I could truly trust. I was tired of being deceived, let down, and lied to. I had been searching for someone or something that I could give my life to that was true and that I could trust. Now I have found it. I could put my life behind it: love, joy, peace, and freedom itself. God Himself, all-powerful, who began to pull me His way even when I was young serving mass, who after I fell into sex, alcohol, and unrighteous living brought me back to Himself.

THE NEXT STEPS

The baptism of the Holy Spirit. I was hooked. God has come into my life and the lives of my girlfriend, Audrey, and two of our friends, Russ and Dee.

We continued to fellowship on Wednesday nights at Light of the Cross. This is when the Holy Spirit began to move on us to change our old ways and come into conformity with his word. We arrived at the altar of sacrifice where our sins were forgiven: the outer court in the Old Testament; the fulfillment in the New Testament. Now we were heading to the inner court, where the altar of the lavar is, where the Holy Spirit has us examine ourselves and convicts us of our old lifestyles and bad habits to bring us to repentance as He begins to transform us into holy people living according to His word.

Truly, old things pass away and all things become new.

I remember going to a Good Friday service at Saint Henry's, the Catholic church where I was raised and served mass. Remember, this was all happening during Lent of 1975.

I was amazed. I spent most of the service in tears of joy and thanksgiving, realizing how much more meaningful this service was now that I'm born again. I remember how much I missed in my life prior to this. Church was so different now that I had a new relationship with Jesus Christ himself.

It seemed like He carried me around on a cloud. I began to share what happened to me with my friends and family. This was a time when the Lord began to shift gears in my life.

We came to a crossroads that, although we continued to fellowship at Light of the Cross, there came a Wednesday night that Russ and Dee were not going. Instead, they invited us up to their house for a drinking party, and Audrey and I were thinking about going. At that point, I was convicted. I knew in my heart this was not something we should do. I was pulled in two different directions—a drinking party with friends or the prayer meeting where my new life began. I had a choice between my old life and my new life.

As I said earlier, God really put a hook on me. This was exactly what I had been searching for, which I now realize is what the rest of mankind is looking for as well.

I could not understand why my friends didn't want to go to the prayer meeting. After much discussion, I figured out that it wasn't that they were never going back to the prayer meeting, just not this week. I, on the other hand, decided that I was going to the prayer meeting. I asked Audrey to take a walk as I wanted to discuss it with her. We went to a nearby park in Arlington called South Side Park. We sat down and I began to share my feelings about going to the prayer meeting. I knew God was calling me and pulling me to go to the prayer meeting and not to the drinking party with Russ and Dee, even though they were our friends in Christ. Looking back, I realize that this was the beginning of a separation from the worldly ways that we were practicing. But at the time, it was choosing the love of God. I think this was one of the first times I began to realize just how much I love Jesus Christ. I shared this with Audrey and gave her the option of coming with me to the prayer meeting or going to the drinking party with Russ and Dee along with other mutual friends.

Audrey said, "I'm coming with you!"

This was one of the first tests I believe we faced in trusting God. This was one of the next steps of leaving the worldly ways for God's ways. It wasn't easy, for we had love for our friends and we had the love of God. This was the beginning of trusting His love. As time worked out, Russ and Dee struggled in their walks, and eventually, Audrey and I began losing many of our friends. We would invite them to go to the prayer meetings, they would invite us to drinking parties, and the separation began.

One night, Audrey and I were looking for something to do. It wasn't that Audrey and I had completely stopped drinking and smoking weed, but that was all about to change that night. We decided to meet at a local bar in Arlington and invite Russ and another longtime friend, Tony, to shoot some pool and have a few beers. We arrived at the bar and ordered a couple of pitchers of beer. Russ and Tony started to rack up the pool table to play some 8 ball when suddenly, I felt the Holy Spirit enter the room. It was only a week prior that Audrey and I went to the Light of the Cross prayer meeting and received the baptism of the Holy Spirit. It was the power of God that suddenly came upon us. I felt strength in my commitment to Christ. It was truly a wonderful experience. This commitment was now at work for us as we were finding our way in this new walk in Christ.

So now I felt this power of God come upon me again while I was in the bar with my friends. Everything stopped. Suddenly, I began to see this bar and what we were doing in a completely different light. I felt the Holy Spirit begin to show me different people in the bar. One should be home with their family, another throwing their money away on alcohol, and another could have been a lawyer but was wasting their life away in drunkenness. It dawned on me as the Holy Spirit put the light on me; I realized I did not belong there.

After much time on the phone with Audrey and our two friends deciding what to do, it was obvious that the Lord did not want us there. Once again it was decision time: Would I obey the Holy Spirit and leave after all this time planning our night, or would I ignore this knowledge and the leading of the Holy Spirit Himself? I was truly convicted as I turned to Audrey and the two pitchers of beer we just bought and said, "I have to leave." Of course, like any couple who just spent an hour deciding what to do tonight, she became very flustered, which I understood.

In consideration of her feelings and since we were all close friends, I trusted her if she wanted to stay, but I knew I would have to leave. I looked at her again and said if she wanted to stay, I would understand, but I was going to leave.

As she looked at me in bewilderment, I turned to Russ and said, "Hey, Russ, I'm going to leave." Russ never even looked at me nor acknowledged my statement. He just kept chalking his cue stick. I then turned to Tony who was racking up the pool table and said the same thing, "Hey, Tony, I'm going to leave." He, just like Russ, never looked at me or acknowledged my statement. It was as if the Lord just pulled a curtain in my life, separating me from this lifestyle and those participating in it.

I looked at Audrey as to what she was going to do. She was shocked about what just happened. These were very close old friends of many years going back to grade school, and she knew something was up. I asked her again what she was going to do, and she responded, "I'm going with you."

We both walked out of the bar. When I got outside, I felt a release and a freedom in my life. God had just delivered me from alcohol. From that day forward, I never got high again either. Whenever I would try to drink a beer or any alcoholic beverage, my body would shut down after two to three beers. I did not desire it like I used to. From that time forward, any time my friends would call me to go hang out and drink, I told them I would not be able to make it. In turn, when the opportunity presented itself, I would invite them to a prayer meeting and testify what God has done for me.

It was during this time that all my friends and many of my family members began to pull away from me. One of my best friends, Ray R., an old drinking buddy and sporty buddy, politely asked me to just drive him home. He proceeded to tell me that he and all my friends in Arlington did not care to be around me anymore. I was talking too much about Jesus.

This was devastating to me; all my friends and my family were pulling away around the same time. Invitations to come over for dinner were disappearing. Much talk was spreading about how much I changed; this was a heavy cross to bear. Although, during this time we did manage to lead a few to the Lord by taking them to the prayer meeting or praying with them on the street. One was my cousin, Sue W., another was my sister-in-law, Sue S., another Audrey's neighbor, Debbie, Bobby B., my mother-in-law Audrey, and my sisters-in-law,

Barb and Mary. God was moving in more ways than one, but I was going through a purging as God was taking me out of the world, delivering me from alcohol, and having to make new friends.

As we continued to fellowship, Audrey was the only one to stick with me. Our relationship was getting serious, and I knew I would need to ask her to marry me or risk losing her as we had been dating for five years. As we continued fellowship at the prayer meeting, the Lord began to convict me of premarital sex. Audrey and I were sexually active, and the Lord was moving in on this. I began to pray about it. I searched the Bible once again regarding it. I talked to other Christians and my minister, Tommy M., about it. The more I talked and sought God's word, the more I realized God was speaking to me. I could not understand that this was a sin, and it was bringing me to another crossroads in my life. What would I love more? God or sex? I was more than concerned about this because I thought if I broke this to Audrey, I would end up losing her, which I did not want to do.

After much deliberation with myself and soul-searching, one night, as we were taking a bath together, I told her how I'd been convicted and that we would have to stop having premarital sex. To much of my surprise, she received it very well and took it as showing her much more respect. Needless to say, I was delighted, as we would still stay together as a couple. To take the edge off our desires for sex, we began reading the book in the Bible, The Song of Solomon, together. We also laid plans to get married as we understood this was God's way for mankind to start a family.

God was rearranging my life. Up till now, I was working for Jerome L. Staab & Sons Inc., of which I was one-fourth of an owner with my three brothers—Gerald, Dave, and Tom. I was also finishing up my second year at Robert Morris College. My professor, Chuck D., had offered me a job at his accounting firm whenever I graduated. He had also helped us incorporate Jerome L. Staab & Sons when my father decided to give the company to his sons.

At this particular time, my father was being audited by the IRS. His bookkeeping was very old school. He basically just used a checkbook. He used to have an accountant from one of his wholesalers come four times a year to do quarterly and year-end tax returns. The

IRS required three years of financial records categorized with financial statements. My father's accountant, who helped with his taxes all along, told my father it was too much for him because of his regular job at the wholesaler. That's when my father asked me if I would be willing to do it for him. How could I say no? My father was a great father to me all these years. I loved him and respected him. He always looked out for those who were in need.

One Christmas Eve, when I was a young boy, he got a no heat call from one of his customers. My father left the Christmas Eve party and went to the customer's house to fix his boiler. It took him a couple of hours. The customer asked how much he owed, and my father responded with, "Merry Christmas." Fifteen or more years later, when I was working at Staab's, this customer came in and told me the story as to why he was sticking with our heating company. It was because of that night over fifteen years ago, the customer told me the story. This wasn't the first time that I encountered firsthand stories of my father's business practices. He was very strong on moral integrity and always treated our customers fair as if their homes were our own.

Many times when I worked for him as a teenager, we would stop at one of the local bars where I lived. The first thing he would do when he went to the bar was to buy the whole bar a drink. Back then many of the men were steel workers and general construction workers, as that's what our neighborhood was primarily made up of. Sometimes, we would stop in our neighborhood at a couple of German clubs, the GBU, or the bierish (beer garden). Many times he would end up singing old German songs and "The Pittsburgh Song," which was one of my favorites. The lyrics were:

> I'll return to the city
> That sets among the hills
> Where the smoke keeps on pouring
> From those good old roaring mills
> And the steamboats in their harbors
> Are going too and fro
> Where the old Allegheny
> And the Monongahela flow

We then arrived home to a made-from-scratch dinner by my mother, Edna. She loved to cook for her five sons—Ron, Gerald, Dave, Tom, and Mike, and my sister, Vivian. I could go on and on about the family hunting and fishing trips at our cottage in Pymatuning. Going snapping turtle fishing with my mother, picking apples, pears, plums, cherries, peaches, and strawberries from her orchard that she would turn into pies and jelly.

I remember coming home with my father and brothers, and as we would pass the exhaust fan from our kitchen, you could smell the pies and all the canning from her huge vegetable garden that I always had the job of turning the ground over for. We would give our two hunting dogs, Penny and Scout, the leftovers and Tippie, our house dog, a good meal.

Needless to say, I took on the project of helping my dad. I took on all the bookkeeping for the last three years he was in business. This was the least I could do for such a great father and mother. My father also began hinting about me coming into the business side of the company. This was another crossroads developing in my life. I had a choice between the offer to join an accounting firm by my professor, which is what I was going to school for, or staying at Staab's. God's plan.

I was one semester from graduating with a two-year associate's degree. My old best friend, Ray, also went to the same college. We used to ride to school together until we had a falling out. As I was working on my father's IRS project, a few things began to change. I was receiving pressure from Audrey regarding our future plans. My father was encouraging me to take over all the accounting duties of our newly formed business as he was retired now and wanted the family to work together.

I had to pray.

These decisions would set me on a path for my future. Certainly, Audrey was in the picture, but I had two more years of college, and getting married now financially would not work. My father, up until now, allowed me to work part-time and go to college even though he turned the business over to the four brothers. My oldest brother, Ronnie, had moved to Pymatuning and owned his own business up there. My sister, Vivian, got married and moved to Pymatuning Lake as well. Although my father, Jerome, turned the business over to his sons, he was still selling jobs and doing some service calls, but he wanted out. I think he admired that I could take care of the administrative side of the business. Even though I had been working in the field, putting in furnaces and air-conditioners and learning the trade, now I had accounting experience. The wheels were turning, and it looked like one of those wheels was running the office.

What should I do?

I loved my brothers, but sometimes they would fight. There was a lot of tension between my brothers and my dad about new ideas. I think that my dad was growing tired; he was now sixty-five years old and waiting to retire from it altogether. Also, the connotation of me, the youngest brother, running the office, while my older brothers have been working their tails off for years in the field, might upset them. I had been part-time for approximately six years and didn't know how they would receive that information.

So now it's decision time. I prayed and felt the Lord was telling me to quit college, get married, and permanently join my brothers in the business. My professor was furious, not only because I was dropping out of college but also because I was going to get married and not join his firm. The funny thing was, the more I trusted what I felt was the Lord's decision and direction for my life, even though I was getting a lot of negative feedback, the freer I felt.

The next step was to talk to my father. He welcomed it with open arms. We talked about my salary, and it looked like things were set for the last leg, which was asking Audrey to marry me. I asked her and, naturally, she said yes. We had been together now for five years, we accepted Jesus Christ and were filled with His Holy Spirit.

It was time to get on with our lives as God was now writing a new chapter. Who would know what was coming next. So much was changed for the good. It was truly amazing.

3

THE CROSS

It's September 1975, and Audrey and I married. It wasn't long before she became pregnant. We had purchased a house on Fitler Street, not far from where we had both grown up in the Arlington neighborhood of Pittsburgh and just a few blocks away from both of our parents. Our lives were surely taking shape in our new lives with the Lord and each other. We were making new friends at Light of the Cross, inviting friends and family to the prayer meetings, and sharing our newfound faith in Jesus Christ. Some were accepting Christ, while others were checking it out.

My mother had come to the Lord. It was funny how that had happened, as my wife and mother-in-law had invited her along with me. When that Wednesday night arrived, I could not make it due to a board meeting at work. I was worried because I thought I had to be there for things to happen. Surely this was the beginning of God breaking my pride. My mother was raised Lutheran and converted to Catholicism after she married my father. She had difficulties in her life. Her mother died when she was only nine years old and she became the caretaker of her younger brothers and father. Then she got married and had six children. Raising a family in the '40s, '50s, and '60s took a toll on her and she had a nervous condition, suffering two nervous breakdowns.

When the board meeting and prayer meeting ended, I was anxious to find out how it all went. They had stopped at my mother-in-law's house after the meeting to have coffee. To my surprise, when I walked in after a rough board meeting, there was my mother beaming from ear to ear. She was full of God's peace to the point that it brought tears to my eyes. Here was a woman, plagued with a nervous condition all her life, who was now filled with God's presence and abundance of His peace. What a gift to me. I remember saying to the Lord if you never did anything again in my life, it was worth it to see my mother walk up her steps covered in God's peace. All the suffering of working, the doctors, and the medications that filled our kitchen cupboards were now basking in God's wonderful hands, the peace that passes all understanding. I was so grateful to the Lord and it was clear that God did not need me to save my mom.

Time was marching on. Audrey was three months pregnant when tragedy struck. Audrey had a miscarriage. It was our first daughter, and I always wanted to call her Rebecca. It was a very hard time, and it felt like the rug had been pulled out from under our feet. The question: Lord, why did this happen? It really challenged our faith. Why would God allow this to happen? It was through this time and the time that followed that the Lord was to introduce me to the cross. The first time was my forgiveness and my salvation. For the longest time in the previous months, God had carried me on his shoulder. I was full of freedom, joy, love, and peace, and I was doing so many wonderful things with family and friends, and now it was a different introduction. It was now time for the Lord to take me off his shoulders, set me on the ground, and tell me to pick up my cross and follow him.

This was a shock, to say the least. Where I was carried through life by the Lord over the past several months, now I had to walk. It took me a while to find my feet, realizing that prayer, reading the word, and fellowship were all necessary things I had to practice to stay close to the Lord. It was a struggle. I came to grips with it all after I realized how Mary lost Jesus at an early age and, again, God was in charge; our first child belonged to him. If he wanted to take her home, that's his prerogative.

Time went on, and Audrey got pregnant again. It was now 1976. Fortunately, this time, God blessed us with a beautiful baby girl whom we named Sarah Ann. Joy once again filled our house with our beautiful daughter. It was truly a learning experience dealing with the suffering in the joy, the valleys, and the mountain tops. I had to learn that life's journey is going to be filled with such; this life is going to be filled with valleys and mountaintops. This was going to be a hard lesson to learn as I was not ready for what was about to come next.

It was 1978, and Audrey's pregnant again. The business was growing rapidly. We have been invited to a Holy Thursday all-night vigil and foot-washing ceremony. Michael K. and Tommy M., both of whom had led me to the Lord, invited us to the service. The service was at the Community of the Crucified One, located in Homestead, Pennsylvania, another steel Town suburb outside of Pittsburgh. It was located in two-row houses converted into an assembly hall. We stayed the whole night. It started with prayer and praise, a message, and a foot-washing ceremony, followed by the reading of the four gospels on the passion and crucifixion of our Lord Jesus Christ throughout the night. With time to pray and meditate on the Lord.

It was now daybreak at 6:00 a.m. Bishop Edward Donovan was the leader of the Community of the Crucified One, a charismatic Christian Church. Bishop Donovan also was currently on the steering committee of the Charismatic movement of the Diocese of Pittsburgh Catholic Church. Bishop Donovan was converted and called to the ministry during a Kathryn Kuhlman service. Kathryn invited him to her Private Bible studies. Bishop Donovan, whom I will call Eddie from now on, was known in many Christian circles for having a healing ministry and for his great insights into the Bible. People from all over would come to hear him preach and pray for healing. People such as Maria Von Trapp and many of her family members would come from Vermont with many others. Also, he would be invited to pray for the sick and preach at many surrounding churches.

Eddie was now going to close the all-night vigil. It was 6:00 a.m. on Good Friday morning. The closing service began with praise.

As we were in the kitchen praising the Lord with Michael K. and Audrey, I began to fall to the floor under the power of God. As I lay there on the floor, it felt like the Lord was peeling all this darkness and sin off of me. As I lay there, I felt peace and grace come upon me. His power came upon me, and I heard His voice for the first time. It seemed as loud as a trumpet as He spoke to me.

He said, "One day, you will lead many through the trials and tribulations of life." He then gave me a prophecy.

While this was happening, the body of Christ and the assembly broke out into tongues. I was a mess crying in great joy as I climbed back off the floor. It was like the Lord had control of my whole being, including my tongue. Just as we pulled ourselves up and stood, the tongues ceased. I gave the prophecies the Lord had given me regarding the end times. I had never done this before, and I was an emotional mess. Then the Lord slayed me again, and I fell to the floor under his power. The church broke out into tongues again as the Lord gave me a second prophecy. Just like before, as we collected ourselves and pulled ourselves up off the floor, the tongues ceased. Just like before, the Lord had control of my being, and I gave a second prophecy. Oddly enough, after the second prophecy, the Lord slayed me a third time and the church broke into tongues.

At this time, I was crying my eyes out, and I felt like a brand-new baby, pure and clean. Meanwhile, the church was going forward to be anointed. We were one of the last ones to be anointed, as it took a while to pull myself together. Audrey and Michael K. were amazed as to what had just happened, as we all were. I had never fallen under the power before and never knew about prophecy. This was all brand new to me. On top of that, even though Eddie was saying *amen, amen* at the end of each prophecy. When I went up to be anointed, he repeated the very words the Lord spoke to me, "I would lead many through the trials and tribulations of life." This was a mindblower.

Truly, the Lord had called me for a purpose that I was not expecting. We went home and slept, as we were up all night at the vigil. My walk with Jesus suddenly took on a new dimension as I was now contemplating his words to me. One of the things he said was, "He is coming soon, even at the door." I remember this word being scripture and having been taught that once Israel became a nation in 1948, all the end-time prophecies before his return would happen in a generation's time. It was Holy Saturday morning when I woke up. Normally, Audrey and I spent the day preparing for Easter Sunday. We usually had our families over for dinner and were preparing for our daughter, Sarah's, second Easter.

No, the Lord had a different plan. After I woke up, the Lord spoke to me and said, "Come to my house." At that time, the only house that I thought he meant was Light of a Cross, which was being held at Tommy M's home where we were attending his Bible studies. So still trying to navigate since "my Paul experience" that my pastor, Tommy M., said I had, I told Audrey what the Lord had said and left for Tommy M.'s house.

I arrived at Tommy's, not knowing why God sent me. Tommy came out of his front door. He was surprised to see me as I did not call him to let him know I was coming. He then asked me what I was doing there. I told him God spoke to me and told me to come to his house.

Tommy then replied, "I'm on my way to Eddie's, the Community of the Crucified One," which is where we were Holy Thursday night. Tommy said that the Lord must want me to come with him, as there was a Holy Saturday service that morning. This was all a giant leap of faith for me. Leaving Audrey at home, preparing for Easter, and being directed by the Lord to come to his house. What are the chances of me catching Tommy just as he was leaving his house? On the way to Eddie's, Tommy shared with me how Light of the Cross, along with Journey's End, another prayer group, were all mission satellites of the Community of the Crucified One, and that Tommy was one of the elders there. So now we were on our way to the motherhouse, as it was called.

I was truly a novice with navigating trying to be obedient to God's spoken word. But it seemed like everything was working out so far. I was putting two and two together, and realizing God knew all the time how I would react. Being in the hands of God was truly exciting, but also scary. I didn't want to screw up. So we arrived at the motherhouse. Eddie was fully vested, blessing, the oils of healing, deliverance, anointing, and holy water. I was taken aback at first seeing the vestments. The last time I saw them was when I left the Catholic church. Again, God was stretching my faith.

In my knowledge, it seemed that the Community of the Crucified One or "the Community" is known as one of the leaders in the charismatic Christian movement. It had strong ties with the Catholic Church but was not under the Catholic church's authority. It was its own entity. It seemed it incorporated all the main elements of the different churches such as Mass and communion from the Catholic churches, along with a third order of Saint Francis, called the chapter, water immersion, baptism for adults, and infant baptism/dedication for infants. It also included the preaching of the word/Bible studies/belief in the gifts of the Holy Spirit and the exercise of them, the concept of being saved by grace through faith, accepting Jesus Christ and his sacrifice on the cross as the personal Lord and Savior, and becoming born again. It seemed like God took all the gifts of the main churches and rolled them into one. There was a lot to this.

We could write a book solely on how God put that all together. There was a lot to absorb, and little did I know that God was planning to move me here one day soon. After meeting several people and receiving the blessed oils and holy water, we had dinner and finally made it back home late in the afternoon. Audrey had done most of the Easter preparations. I took time to explain all that went on in my day. She was very receptive but very curious as to what was happening in our lives. It was a lot to absorb. I helped her finish some of the preparations, which wasn't much, and then we all sat down and sampled the Easter ham with ham sandwiches, potato, and macaroni salad, our new family tradition.

It was spring 1978, and God was moving in our lives. The Lord had called me to a deeper walk under a deep subjection to His Holy Spirit. Part of His direction to me was that "He would send people to me, and to only speak the words He would give me." It sounded like a pretty large restriction, but I found great freedom in it. As I went through my daily life, there were times when God would move through me, sometimes to say nothing at all, and other times to speak his words to whomever. He had also given me the discernment to tell what was troubling people even though they would say nothing or talk about something completely different. The Holy Spirit was teaching me how to minister to the hurt, the lost, and the oppressed. He also brought me insight into His word.

One day as I was picking up a birthday card at a local store, I was standing in line at the checkout. Suddenly, the Holy Spirit began to move on me, and He spoke to me saying to ask the checkout lady if she knew the Lord. This was now a new phase of ministry for me, to boldly ask the question to a stranger who was ringing me up to buy a birthday card. Also, there were three other people standing in line behind me. All these things were going through my mind as God was asking me to step out in faith for Him. I was also wondering what these people behind me might think as they were waiting to check out. What would the clerk think?

I started praying, trying to make sure this was the Lord asking me to do this. I know I had been taught that God would never direct you to break His word. I also remembered the scripture in the Bible that says we should be willing to be a fool for Christ. All these things were going through my head at light speed as I was deciding whether or not I was going to pop the question. This type of thing might be easy for some, but risking total embarrassment was difficult for me. Again, the question hit me. How much do I love the Lord? I remembered a scripture that says, "If you profess me before men, I will profess you to my Father and the angels." Well, that did it for me.

As I approached her, I laid the card down on the counter and I asked her the words the Lord gave me. "Do you know the Lord?"

The woman, who was in her '50s, looked at me and said, "I always wanted to pray for that."

Under the direction of the Holy Spirit, I respond with, "Do you want me to pray with you now to ask the Lord into your heart?"

She responded yes. So we took hands while the people in line were waiting and watching, and we prayed. We asked the Lord Jesus to come into her heart and forgive her sins. She began to weep and followed with a huge smile on her face. At the same time, she began thanking me for praying with her as she began to ring me up for the card. I responded with "God bless you," glorifying and thanking God for the miracle.

I left the store with great joy. I realized the people behind us never said a word. God was in control the whole time, and His words bore fruit. Through this time, as God was using me to step out in faith in His word, my confidence and trust in Him grew. Each time He gave me a word or a direction, it came to pass or bore fruit.

Another time during this period, I was working in my garage, doing some maintenance, when my neighbor Fred stopped down to see me. Fred retired in his '70s. He was a great guy, always willing to help with a project. That day, we began talking. His wife would always go to a local church on Sunday but not Fred. We began to talk. I began to learn how the Holy Spirit can lead a conversation with Jesus. We were talking about what I was doing when the next thing I knew, we simply were sharing how simple salvation is. It is not about just going to church, but it is the church's responsibility to lead you to Christ, to lead you to ask His forgiveness and to form a personal relationship with Him. He is real, and He loves you and died for you.

Needless to say, the Holy Spirit moved in, and Fred was all ears. I then simply asked Fred if he would like to pray and ask the Lord Jesus Christ into his heart. He said yes, and we prayed. As we prayed, the Lord entered his heart. He was beaming with God's light on him with a smile from ear to ear, filled with God's love and joy. He quietly expressed his gratitude and joy when he left and walked home. I was so excited about what just happened. Jesus saved Fred. I went up to my house to share the good news with Audrey. Her cousin, Cecelia, was visiting with Audrey.

As I burst into their conversation after greeting Cecelia, I began to share what had just happened. Cecelia was all ears. At the end of telling them what just happened with the Lord and Fred, Cecelia looked up to me from the kitchen table where she was sitting and asked me would you pray with me too? Of course, I said yes. Audrey had just been talking with her about some problems Cecelia was going through. We took hands, and Cecelia asked the Lord in her heart. She had tears of joy and great relief as if someone lifted the world off her back. It was truly a jubilation. God was moving in my garage, my kitchen, and at the store. Cecelia was filled with tears of joy as she left our house that day. We were awestruck.

What was God going to do next? Well, it didn't take long to find out. The following week, the preacher's program was opened up at the Community of the Crucified One, the church where God slayed me in the spirit and called me to lead many through the trials and tribulations of life. God anointed me. I felt the calling in my life to preach God's word and serve him.

I was married, and Audrey just gave birth to our daughter Kellie, which was such a big blessing to all of us. We were so filled with joy, another beautiful daughter. I owned and had a full-time job at Staab's, managing and running the business with my brothers. The business was doubling in growth each year. Then I faced another crossroads in my life. Certainly, God has had other plans for my life from the beginning. Now another change was on its way.

It was now late fall in 1978, and the preacher's program was opening in the Community. I was still fellowshipping at the Light of the Cross, where I found the Lord. There, I was tithing and joined their building ministry. Tommy, the pastor, was preparing to expand the ministry and wanted to add to his house so he did not have to rent a hall for services. My commitment was now expanding. Besides the duty at Light of the Cross, which was my storehouse for the Lord, the Lord was now adding to the preacher's program.

Upon entering the preacher's program, Eddie informed us of all of the requirements. We had to believe we were called to preach, either as an evangelist or a pastor. We had to attend his Bible studies on Friday night. We had to also attend the preacher's class that he taught on Saturday nights. We had to memorize three thousand verses of the Bible. We would recite ten to fifteen verses a week to an elder after the Friday night Bible study. We had to summarize the whole Bible and submit ten chapters a week that Eddie himself would review and grade. We had to preach twenty sermons and be critiqued by Eddie and the class. We had to join a ministry in the Community, which, at the present time, the service ministry at Light of the Cross would fulfill. That later evolved into us joining one at the Community as well.

As time went on, the Community was expanding, building Mission houses throughout Homestead, Clairton, the suburbs of Pittsburgh, and throughout the United States: Vermont, Cleveland, California, and Chicago to name a few. I donated my talent to the heating and air-conditioning business. This was how I got to know Eddie personally. He asked me if I would be willing to work on the furnace at the motherhouse, which, at the beginning, there were only two.

Over time, this led to forty-six furnaces and numerous air-conditioners. This also led to fixing the plumbing, washer and dryers, refrigerators, and freezers. This was a time in my life when I had to learn how to balance my job, my family, and my calling to the ministry. As responsibilities began to grow, Audrey became pregnant again. At the same time, my mother, Edna, had fallen ill with leukemia. Tensions begin to flare up. Where would I draw the line? First, it became evident that serving the Lord at the Light of the Cross was becoming too much. Other members of the preacher's program were experiencing this as well. I had to pray. What was God saying to me? I felt like I had to be in two places at the same time. Both ministries were expanding, and so were conflicting schedules.

Tension grew. Some of the members at the Light of the Cross left to go to the Community, which created tensions between the pastors. I was torn. Light of the Cross was my home. I could not imagine leaving, for God had so blessed me. More and more brothers and sisters were moving to the community. Up until now, I felt committed to the Light of the Cross. Then the Lord spoke to me. He directed me to talk to Tommy and ask him how he felt if my family moved to the Community, as I felt God began drawing me there to begin a new chapter in my life. I didn't want to leave the Light of the Cross, even after so many had left.

On another step in faith, I sat down with Tommy. He believed it was God's will for me to move to the community. To be a tither at the Community, you had to fill out a request form. It would then be brought to the elder's meeting and voted upon. Everyone and anyone was always welcome to the services at the Community, but to become a tither by money, service, time, or prayer, you had to be accepted. Elder's meetings were held once a month. I submitted my application and received a response in one day to my surprise. I was accepted. My family and I would now be a part of the Community of the Crucified One, of which Tommy was an elder.

This was a great relief to me, as now I received confirmation from my pastor and the Community. I don't know how it got approved so fast, but it was helping me to better balance my life with all of the responsibilities. I believe this was God's hand moving in my life. Although this direction by the Lord helped, it still was not easy, with a growing family, growing company, trying to keep up with my studies, and the ministry that was growing very quickly. I had to grow as well. This was one of the crosses, and the sacrifice that goes with it became my next challenge.

One of the hardest things that I ever had to do through my journey with the Lord was to leave my newly formed family at home when God was calling me out the door to work, to serve God, and to other places. God blessed me with such a beautiful family, who I love very much. I would pray each and every time I would be called to leave to make sure of God's will. Serving God begins at home. I would struggle with tears in my prayer time, as many times it didn't make sense to go. I wanted to make sure I was doing God's will. So I made a deal with the Lord. I'll pay the price, but you bless my kids and be with them since I cannot be here with them all the time.

SACRIFICE AND THE CROSS

Surely life was changing and changing fast. It was now 1980, and my wife had just given birth to my son, Matthew Michael. Another huge blessing: a beautiful son. We had great joy, our family was growing, but at the same time, my mother was dying. I was having difficulty balancing the joy with the sorrow. I had to put on numerous hats—father, husband, owner of a business ministry preachers program, son, and brother. It became very difficult for me to change hats so quickly to fulfill the requirements that were being asked of me. I realized God was molding me. I found myself up late at night, trying to balance and fit everything together. I began to backslide.

Although Eddie had given me much encouragement, along with Audrey, Tommy, and fellow classmates, I, in turn, was losing my grip on the Lord. As I look back, I realize I was wrestling with the cross and the suffering in my life. Particularly, I was wrestling with the sacrifice it was going to take to balance everything. Many of my classmates who were in the preacher's program were dropping out. Out of about thirty-five of us in the beginning, there were only twenty left after two years. Eddie used to say it was his job to push us out. That if we were truly called, God would make a way for us to finish the program. We had to be willing to put God first, or we would be useless as a preacher. When the class would complain about not getting enough sleep because of all of the requirements, he advised us to get God involved and ask Him to multiply our sleep.

My mother died on August 2, 1980. This was so difficult to face. Our family was devastated. It was like someone dropped an atomic bomb in the middle of our family. It broke my heart as I had loved her dearly. I was falling under the heavy weight of it all. I started having anxiety attacks, which led to problems at work. My marriage was struggling, and I was struggling with the ministry. I was only in the book of Psalms in my summarizations. It had been two years.

Other classmates, who had been laid off from their work or were able to devote more time to the ministry, were able to earn credits toward their summarizations, memorization, and sermons. They earned credits during the building in the expansion of the mission houses. We were required to put eight hours a week in as a part of the preacher's program. After the first eight hours, any additional hours could be used toward a summary or any of the other requirements. This was designed to teach us about the time necessary to be a pastor. You had to learn to balance, not to abandon your family or responsibilities, but to sacrifice. Because of all of my responsibilities, I didn't have extra time to earn extra credits. Therefore, I had to do all of the work.

Since I was becoming a preacher, I was determined that I knew what was in the Bible. Therefore, I didn't want to use credits to skip a summary. It was discouraging, though, seeing some of my fellow classmates excel, while I was stuck, grinding it out day by day. I came to the conclusion that I had no time for myself. My time was divided between my job, my family, and my ministry. I always made it a point to be home for dinner. Wednesday nights were spent with the kids, along with Sunday afternoons and a mix of different times in between work and ministry.

Eddie taught us many things as we journeyed through different sections of the Bible, which helped me tremendously. But my biggest problem was the sacrifice. To top things off, in the 1980s, the steel mills began to collapse, which put the economy into a recession. Money became so tight. It was just another weight on my shoulders, for the business was now struggling. Things got so bad that Audrey began to say that she did not recognize me.

As the tensions had caught up with our marriage, I began to feel oppressed by the enemy. It seemed on every front in my life that I thought I was going to have a nervous breakdown. It got so bad. I was scared, and I was beginning to feel like the Lord was abandoning me. It was here that I experienced my darkest moment in life. Everything seemed like it was falling apart. I began to realize that I was running from the crosses in my life. My mind was saying one thing and my heart, another. I became stalled in the preacher's program, along with the other areas of my life. I realized that I was trying to find a way around the cross, and God was not having it. So methodically, God began to strip me. I had lost my peace. We were fighting and wrestling on every front. I had no joy, just misery and oppression. This went on for almost a year.

I finally realized God's callings are without repentance. It was his way or who knows, maybe a mental hospital. I remember standing in front of my refrigerator one day at home. I cried out to the Lord and said, "Anything is better than this." I was afraid that the cross would be misery, but I was already living in it. It was my submission to do his will and live his way. It seemed like the most lame submission and commitment.

I remember thinking if I were God, I think I would say, "Hit the road, Jack," but He didn't. It seemed like almost instantly, the anxiety was lifted, and peace began to filter into my heart. I was so happy as this misery was lifting. I began to realize how fortunate I was by just having peace and not being haunted by oppressive thoughts.

Slowly, my walk was rebounding, and my perspective was clearing as I picked up my crosses and decided, "Your way, Jesus, not mine." I learned a lot about the cross and suffering during these difficult times. I began to understand God's word, that true life, abundant life, and the treasures of life are about learning how to embrace our cross and carry our cross. It helped me to realize that, as I was accepting God's will over my stubborn will, something was happening. I was becoming less selfish. I was just dying in my old sinful nature as my new nature in Christ was growing. Joy and peace in

God's love were growing in my heart. The long-suffering of carrying the crosses in my life became a springboard to walk in the liberty of God's Holy Spirit. I felt freedom from sin and guilt, embracing God's presence in a stronger and more intimate way. Everything was coming back together again.

Whereas thinking the cross the Lord was asking me to pick up was all misery, I realize now it is the answer to life itself. Many scriptures became alive to me, such as Matthew 10:38, where Jesus said that if we are not willing to pick up our cross and follow him, we are not worthy of him. In Luke 9:23, He said, "To deny yourself, take up your cross daily and follow me." Suddenly, this all became alive to me. It was the key to life itself. So many run away from the cross, throw it down as I did, or look for another way around the cross.

Without dying in our selfish sinful nature, we would never find what Christ truly meant when he spoke of abundant life, God's will transform us from the fears, doubts, anxieties, and depressions of this world. So many things came together for me having gone through this time. Christ was truly teaching me about life and how to get through the trials and tribulations of life. I remembered my original calling, that I would lead many through the trials and tribulations of life. Little did I know that some of the greatest trials I would ever have to face were yet to come.

5

ORDINATION AND THE
MISSION FIELD

It's 1983, and I finished all of my preacher's program requirements. Eddie, our bishop, had an art at presenting and pushing us preacher students to the cross. For example, just as I was finishing my summarizations of the books of the Bible, I was in the Epistles of 1 John 1, 2, and 3. Up till now when summarizing the previous books that had many more chapters to cover, I was averaging about fifteen handwritten pages for approximately ten chapters. I was identifying the keys, the most important parts of the overall meaning of those chapters, and always moving along smoothly. I was getting decent grades, and my eyes were upon finishing this marathon that began over five years prior. One hope was to finish before summer, so I would be eligible for ordination that was held in August.

When I began to summarize 1 John, it only had five chapters. I handed in a summary that had seven pages, half of what I usually handed in on ten chapters. For the first time in five years, I received it back with the note "not enough." I proceeded to do it over, thinking Eddie our bishop wanted more input- I handed in fifteen pages. Again, I got that back marked "not enough." I was starting to feel perturbed. He knew I was pushing to get done. The last leg of the program is in sight. I figured this was another test. This went on three more times with the same book, 1 John. I handed in a summary with twenty pages, then twenty-five pages. Finally, when I handed in thirty-five pages, for a grand total of seventy pages, he gave me a *fair grade*.

Until now, I always received good or excellent grades. I was thinking, *Really?* The next book, 2 John, only has one chapter with thirteen verses. How many pages should I start out with? You would think I would have realized what Eddie was doing, but I didn't. I handed in five pages on thirteen verses and got back "not enough." So do I bite the bullet and hand in thirty-five pages on one chapter, or play the game of writing a total of seventy pages that I just went through with 1 John? I jumped to fifteen pages and, again, got back the note, "not enough." This was killing me.

Just when I thought I would get some kind of break, there was yet another hardship. I easily summarized the whole Bible until now. Eddie had passed and ordained some of my fellow classmates who breezed through the program on credits earned through working on the mission house buildings. But there I was, grinding it out, having done all these summaries, and he required more. When you run a marathon and you see other racers passing by on a golf cart, you understand the fact that life is unfair, and it can be very discouraging. Especially when you think you've reached the downhill point in a marathon, suddenly it becomes uphill. Yet I began to think, "So what?" I took my eyes off my classmates and Eddie and decided that I was glad I summarized the whole Bible. I put in the work and did not breeze through on credit. After all, I needed to know about the Bible if I was going to be a preacher. I decided to take the time element out of the equation. It was something I had to deal with all along, bringing Christ into it, and asking for his grace to overcome.

Once again, I realized that he helped me by handing me a cross to kill my pride, which I had a lot of, and move into the freedom of doing it just for Jesus. I was not giving up. I gave a total of twenty-five pages on 2 John, 3 John, Jude, and Revelations, and I was done! Praise the Lord. I felt that by going through this preacher's program for the past five years, I learned so much about the Word and myself. I think going through this at the same time as having a family, a job, and now a calling to preach the gospel was the hardest thing I've ever done.

The most important lesson I learned, which I don't think I ever would have unless I was put in life's pressure cooker, was about the cross that liberated me from myself. The cross helped me step into a different dimension with grace and selflessness. It helped me walk into God's will, while at the same time developing a closer walk with Jesus Christ and finding what and where abundant life truly is. I experienced Christ's freedom in the Holy Spirit, and his love, joy, peace, and, even suffering. I've learned to embrace the cross in my life, pick them up, and carry them. I enjoy my family and friends in such a way that would not be possible without him. Truly, I found the key to life, and it matches the word of God: it's the Cross.

I just didn't know how to get there, but I thank God, in his Holy Spirit, Eddie, and everyone else along the way who pushed me to the cross so that I could discover selflessness. I discovered the self-lessness that Christ exhibited on the cross when He said He would show me the way. Our world promotes selfishness, pride, and ambi-tion and sees the cross as foolish. If the world only knew that what they are looking for in freedom, liberty, love, joy, and peace is truly found at the cross. They are found in Jesus, the source and the author of true freedom, liberty, and eternal life.

Once I finished the summaries of the Bible, as well as the ser-mons, memorizations, studies, and work on the mission houses, I had to prepare for a trial sermon. To be ordained, I needed to com-plete the entire program. I also had to give a public trial sermon. To be ordained, there had to be God's stamp of approval on it. That means that, during the service, there had to be two supernatural signs or wonders, such as healing, salvation, or some movement of God. All signs and wonders, along with the sermon, were to be judged by superiors and elders who moved through the crowd, watching and listening, recording any such events.

After the sermon, the determination about whether or not God moved during the service was made by the elders and supe-riors assigned. So the heat was on. The elders scheduled my trial sermon, and I had a week to prepare. We, meaning the Holy Spirit and myself, began by praying to the Lord for a scripture that he wanted us to preach upon. I should've had more faith than I did. Since God brought me that far, he surely wasn't going to drop me. The Lord gave me the scripture Matthew 1:5, the Genealogies, that reads: "Salmon the father of Boaz whose mother was Rahab, Boaz the father of Obed whose mother was *Ruth*, Obed the father of Jesse…" The Genealogies for a trial sermon? Was I hearing the Lord right? I wrestled with this because surely there were so many other juicy scriptures. The scripture might have been a burden to spark the interest of the crowd. Nevertheless, I learned from Peter in the scripture: when Jesus wanted him to go back out on the sea and fish after a night of no luck, Peter obeyed the Lord and caught many fish. So nevertheless, your will, Lord!

I prepared the sermon under the direction of the Holy Spirit, who wanted me to focus on Ruth. Ruth was a gentile and a nobody, yet we find her in the genealogy bloodline of Jesus. Well, the trial sermon day arrived. I was pretty nervous, and with everything on the line for ordination, I prayed for the Lord to show up and get me through.

We began the service, and I preached that Ruth was a nobody, yet we found her in the bloodline of Jesus. God has a plan for you! After the service, we had to wait in the office until a determination was made as to whether or not there were any signs and wonders during the service. I think it was one of the longest waits of my life. Finally, Elizabeth Clare, a superior, and Howard, an elder, came into the office. They reported that a woman named Rosemary received a back healing. Another person named Ruth was in the audience. She was visiting the Community with a group from Vermont and came to the Lord through the message. Who would know that God was sending another Ruth from Vermont to the sermon about Ruth? I'm glad I trusted in the Lord. Needless to say, I passed. We praised and thanked the Lord for guiding me. From that day on, I learned to trust the Lord and his word. His word always bears fruit or touches somebody.

6

ASSIGNMENTS

One of the church programs that developed over this period was the priesthood program. The priesthood program consisted of advanced learning for those ordained as pastors or evangelists who felt a calling to perform the Catholic sacraments such as holy communion, extreme function, and confession. If you were ordained as a pastor or evangelist, the gospel permitted you to perform marriages, baptisms, and funerals. This caused concern for the Catholic Church Diocese, who cited the succession of Peter and the handing down of the Eucharist through that succession, claiming the Eucharist was for Catholics only. Through much deliberation, the Community of the Crucified One believed the Eucharist or Holy Communion was for everyone who believed in Jesus Christ. That group included Baptists, Lutherans, Methodists, Pentecostals, and anyone who believed in Jesus Christ. This subject is what divides the Christian church today in their theology.

As a youth, Eddie learned of the Catholic beliefs in seminary. Through witnessing numerous signs and wonders as an adult, he believed his calling was to help bring the Christian churches together. As the Bible tells us, one day, Christ's church will be without a spot or wrinkle. All the gifts that Christ left us will be in one church. Finally, the Catholic church decided to leave the Community alone and that it would treat it like every other denomination.

Needless to say, I faced a decision as I was born and raised Catholic. But no one truly introduced me to Jesus until I came to the Light of the Cross and the Community of the Crucified One. In those days and days to follow, there were numerous healings, salvations, and baptisms of the Holy Spirit. Roman Catholic nuns, Baptist ministers, and people from all denominations were being healed. One nun received a brand-new lung after it was surgically removed years before. Another secretary of the Catholic bishop, Lenard, received a healing of growth on the side of her neck. These were documented by the medical profession and could not be denied. God's stamp of signs and wonders follow those who believe. God was definitely present, so I decided to join both the Third Order of Saint Francis, called the chapter, and the priesthood program.

If you remember in an earlier chapter, when I was in eighth grade, serving Mass with Father Bench, I wanted to be a priest. The great thing about the Community was that you could be a priest and be married as well. I believe this was all a part of God's plan for my life. I grew to enjoy the doctrine of the Community, as it resembled the early church. Peter, the first priest after our Lord and King, was married. The chapter vows were spiritual vows. I could spend a lot of time explaining all about this, but primarily it was designed for laypeople. You could be married, divorced, or single and still grow into a deeper walk with Jesus Christ.

The priesthood program largely surrounded administering the sacrament of baptism, Holy communion, baptism of the Holy Spirit, marriage, holy orders, and extreme unction. All of these circled around the salvation experience of receiving Christ as your Lord and Savior and the forgiveness of your sins to receive eternal salvation. The program also included insights into counseling, other religions, and beliefs of the world. It was an extensive program grounded in the word of God. The program consisted of receiving teachings and taking notes. Teachings occurred one weekend a month when we would be taught on a Friday night and all day Saturday. This program also prepared us to lead a church, teaching us administrative skills. The

Community was expanding, with the addition of numerous mission houses.

During this time, new mission houses and churches were springing up throughout the country in places like California, Chicago, Cleveland, Erie, Clairton, New Jersey, Vermont, and New York. New mission houses were planted as members of the Community moved to these different areas and requested the possibility of starting a mission house there. The members would start a prayer meeting which would grow into a new mission house. This mission house would be an extension of the Community. Opportunities began to develop and I was permitted to apply to relocate as a pastor at these locations as they became available.

My first assignment was to travel to Erie Pennsylvania, 120 miles away, to conduct a prayer meeting once a week. There were two members of the Community who moved there and were trying to plant a mission house by starting a prayer meeting. Prior to this, I had applied to go to California or Erie after much prayer in discussions with my wife, Audrey. The elders decided Erie was a better fit for me as I could commute once a week until a congregation was established. This lasted for about a year; I would leave Pittsburgh on Thursday afternoons, conduct a prayer meeting, and travel home that night.

On occasion, my father, Jerome, would accompany me on this trip. A lot of wheels were turning in those days. The Clairton, Pennsylvania mission house, called Saint Claire was growing and they needed an assistant pastor. No one wanted the job. Eddie asked me if I would be willing to transfer from the mission house in Erie back to Pittsburgh to take the assistant pastor position at Clairton. I could commute from my present home, for it was only thirty minutes away from Clairton. It made a lot of sense. If I moved to another state, I would have to divest myself from the heating company and open up a branch office. This would have required a lot of planning, house-hunting, and a large investment. I was planning all of these things in my spare time. I look back now and believe Eddie had other things in mind for me. I prayed about it, Audrey was agreeable, and so we took the position in Clairton. Joe W. was the pastor. We actually grew up in the same area and I knew Joe very well. He accepted this assignment a few years prior. We got along very well.

At the Clairton church, one of my duties was to cut the grass. I prayed for a riding lawnmower, and God answered my prayer in the first month. It made life a lot easier. I served there for about two years when, one day, as I was performing maintenance on the lawnmowers, I felt like someone was watching me. When I looked up, Eddie was in his car about fifty yards away, just watching me. Soon after, he pulled away. I wondered why he sat there just watching me. Little did I know, something was soon going to change.

The Clairton mission house grew rapidly during our stay, and I was learning firsthand about being a pastor. We ministered to a lot of people on service days, but the majority of my time those years involved maintenance on both Clairton and all of the Pittsburgh houses. Something was beginning to unfold regarding my talents, not only in the ministry field, but also in the heating, plumbing, and air-conditioning field.

During this time, Audrey became pregnant again and gave birth to our fourth child in May 1985, Elizabeth Mary. We now had another beautiful daughter who brought us extreme joy as our family was growing. The children were growing as well. We had a full house and all the blessings that come with a new arrival. I felt really blessed. God was setting up our lives and changes were about to come.

It was November 1987. Each year, all the ministers gathered at the motherhouse on the Feast of Christ, the King to celebrate the priesthood, which included all the pastors, assistant pastors, evangelists, and priests. During the service, we would recommit our lives to the Lord and the preaching of the gospel. We would line up in order and process into the service as part of the ceremony.

Just before the beginning of the ceremony, one of the priests approached me and said that Eddie was going to raise me as his assistant pastor during the service. I would no longer be the assistant pastor at Clairton. This was a shock. I would be assistant pastor to the bishop. I always tried to do my best unto the Lord, balancing my family, the ministry, preaching, and working on furnaces, gas lines, washers, dryers, etc. Now God was raising me up to be the bishop's assistant pastor. I was flabbergasted. I think everyone else was shocked as well. Surely, there were others who many thought should be put in that position. I had large shoes to fill, not only spiritually but physically as well.

We had dinner after the service. It took a while for me to get changed and navigate through many who congratulated me. When I walked into the hall, Eddie introduced me as his new assistant pastor and asked everyone to move to make room for me to sit at the head table. I was overwhelmed with gratitude and humility. Moving down one seat didn't sit well with some of my fellow ministers, who right away started wondering if I had authority over them. This was another test of trusting the Lord. I began to wonder if I could fill the shoes of this position and also gain the respect of my peers.

Well, it didn't take long for the story of Joseph and his brothers to take effect. When I talked to Eddie after the dinner, he told me that he wanted me to do the Thursday night service at the motherhouse. Also, I had to see him at his office whenever I came and when I left on a daily basis. There were many other duties associated with this position, including maintaining order within the several mission houses surrounding the motherhouse, the school, and the main church building. There was a lot of traffic at the motherhouse every day.

Another duty that Eddie gave me was security. The community was in the heart of a ghetto. There were lots of shootings, stabbings, and thefts. Because of this environment, Eddie was concerned about the protection of all the people living in all the different buildings, including the motherhouse. Too many times doors were left unlocked. Eddie wanted me to check all the doors at eleven each night. I wrestled with this request. There were at least thirty full-time residents living in these houses, at least half of whom were male adults.

Surely, one of the men who lived there could make rounds and check the doors at night. I questioned Eddie about this, and no matter what other suggestions I came up with, Eddie was convinced that I was the one who should do it. At first, I didn't understand and it didn't make sense to me. My family did not like it either. Of course,

I understood their frustrations, because it did not make sense to me either. I had to pray. This was difficult for me. With a growing family, leaving them every night, rain or shine, to go to the middle of a ghetto was not ideal.

Audrey was concerned for my well-being along with the interruption of our nights together. I prayed and prayed. I thought that certainly, God would not expect this when there were others living at the facilities, but I was wrong. For whatever reason, I felt that the Lord wanted me to do this. I know man can make mistakes and we should follow God. Eddie was my superior, my boss, and my bishop. So I asked God to confirm His will in this matter. God is big enough to confirm his will. In addition to all of these concerns, the Crips and the Bloods, two rival gangs, lived within a block of the community. Eddie bought me a stun gun for protection, as he was concerned for me. Well, here we go. I grew up in Arlington, a very rough neighborhood. I had been in many fights in my younger days, so I could take care of myself. In my prayer time, the Lord made it clear to me that this was his will, but I wanted to be sure this was the Lord. I still asked for confirmation.

As I began to step into this responsibility by faith, a number of things began to take shape surrounding this late-night adventure. One night, it was a priesthood weekend and I had to leave a lot earlier to make it in time for the teaching. I would stay until 11:00 p.m. to lock up. Well, here came the test. My whole family was upset and crying that I was leaving early. We used to have such a great time with each other; the Holy Spirit used to inspire me with different things to play with the kids.

I would give them different kinds of rides as if we were at an amusement park; one was "the elevator ride," where I would pick them up, lift them up simulating going up an elevator, stopping at different floors on the way up till their heads touched the ceiling. Then I would say, "Basement!" and quickly drop them down to the floor. Another was called "back to the future" ride. They would hop on my back like a piggyback ride. I would then back up slowly, make a noise like a rocket engine, come to a stop, and then make a noise like a rocket explosion and run with them throughout the house.

Also, there was "the sugar foot" ride, among many others, that the kids just loved. It seemed to me that although I was out of the house a lot, the times that were spent together were so great that I knew the Lord was blessing us. So this was one of these nights, but they didn't want me to leave as we were having such a wonderful time.

Audrey was upset, and here I was getting ready to walk out the door, leaving a perfect family who loved me. It was so very difficult. It was during times like these that I questioned if I was doing God's will. It was heart-wrenching, I always prayed, and I knew he wanted me to go. I didn't understand it, but I knew it was the Lord's will. I remember that as I was walking out that night, I asked myself why would God want me to leave them. Everyone was crying and upset because they loved me and wanted me to stay. I remember the deal I made with the Lord many years ago, that if I were to live according to His will, He would bless and keep my family. I walked out the door with tears in my eyes. I felt like Abraham, ready to sacrifice his son, Isaac. I got in my car and proceeded to the Community.

When I was one block away, I realized I had forgotten my Bible and notebook for the teaching. Eddie would not let you in the class without your Bible. I dreaded going back home to get it. It was hard enough watching them cry when I left and now I had to go back. As I entered the front door, having left only minutes before, my family was laughing. At first, I thought I was seeing things. Surely they were crying as I left them, but now they were laughing. At first, I was going to become mad that they just put me through so much distress to now be laughing minutes later. I was going to say something, but then I felt the Holy Spirit speak to my heart, saying, "Just get your Bible." I did as He said and just got my Bible. It was as if they never saw me come back, even though I walked through the living room where they were all sitting. I didn't say a word and walked out the door again.

As I closed the door, the Lord stopped me on my front porch and spoke to me. He said, "When you walked out, I walked in. I have your family." Faith is the evidence. This was the first of confirmations the Lord gave me regarding leaving my family to go lock up "God's house." God began moving through these nights of lock-up. I started bumping into a woman who only lived a block away while we were checking and locking doors. She was a battered wife with black eyes and bruises. We talked, and I would minister to her and counsel her. She had a habit of walking her dog around the same time I was locking up. She became a member of the church, and God freed her from her husband. There was not a night that I did not spend ministering to the residents who lived there, someone passing on the street, or someone visiting from the out-of-town mission houses. It was a silent ministry in the middle of the night. Sometimes, I would not get home until 1:00 a.m.

Most nights, as I prepared to leave, Eddie wanted me to check in with him. He would talk with me many times, sometimes for over an hour. We would talk about what was going on in my life, the ministry, and different people in the ministry. I truly treasured these talks when we would have them late into the night. It gave me great insight into the ministry in my own life. It grounded me and helped me balance my life.

Being his assistant also involved traveling with Eddie when he was invited to be a guest speaker at other churches. We acted as security along with other pastors, Buzz and Father Paul. He also would have us open the service with an opening prayer or scripture. The times I valued most, besides being a part of the services, was being with him when he would talk with other famous preachers. He talked with people like Russ and Norma Bixler, who started Christian broadcast TV stations, Evelyn Carter, Archie Dennis, a world-known evangelist and singer, Isaac Greene, and Pastor Tunie.

All of whom were men and women of God. I would learn so much about ministry from listening to their conversations with each other. Also, I valued just getting to know them and interacting with their families or members of their churches. God was using the late-night lock-up in more ways than one. God was showing me that not everyone could talk to Eddie in the way I did. It was obvious that God brought me under Eddie's wing, to learn from him and help him in many ways. What an honor! I knew it didn't come without a price. I understand now that the Lord set up this time I had with Eddie. God had called me to lead many through the trials and tribulations of life, and I would need someone like Eddie to help me learn how to do that. God would have to take me through trials and tribulations if I were to ever lead someone else.

7

DELIVERANCES
AND HEALINGS

It's the late 1980s and the steel mills in Pittsburgh are crashing. The economy is bad. Our heating business is failing. I hurt my back carrying air-conditioners at the Community mother's house. I could not pick up a garbage bag and was bent over like an elderly man. It hurt so much. Right around the same time, I received word from the Lord, through Eddie, that I was going to be going through a hard time but God will get me through it. After that word, we got a call from the IRS.

Due to the economic climate, we were losing money at the heating company. We fell behind in our payroll taxes along with the state and local taxes. We owed the IRS $186,000. I was the secretary-treasurer of our company. We saw it coming, and we knew we owed it. We were just having a couple of bad years, but the taxes mounted up to this large total. We agreed to set up a meeting with the IRS and our attorneys. At the same time, Eddie was having a miracle service in downtown Pittsburgh that he would do once a month. I decided to go as one who needed healing. The miracle service started.

Midway through the service, Eddie called out for anyone with back problems to come to the front. I went up, and he turned me around, putting his hand on my back. As he did, it felt like strings were being tied in my back. A warmth came upon me at the same time. He turned me back around, touched my forehead, and I fell down to the floor under the power of God. When I got up, my back was healed.

After the service, I went back to work, and my nephew was unloading cement pads off our stake bed truck. I thought that if God truly healed me, I should be able to help him unload them. I did it with no problem. My clothes dryer at home was broken, so when I got home, I carried in my toolbox and fixed my dryer that had a broken belt with no problem. God really healed me. It reminded me that back in 1976, when I had a very bad headache and had never experienced a miracle before, I asked the Lord to heal my headache. I put my hands on my head and asked him to heal me. Instantly, my headache lifted. I never had a headache again, but now I was facing a much larger problem, a $186,000 problem. My brothers and I, along with our $200-an-hour lawyer, set a date to meet with the IRS. We met up with the IRS agent named Bart. He sat across a long table from us, smoking a cigarette, asking how we were planning to pay.

Our lawyer began to speak as my brother and I sat frozen in our chairs. As I listened to our lawyer talk, it seemed like he had marbles in his mouth. Nothing was making sense, and we were getting nowhere fast. The tensions grew as I was praying to the Lord to deliver us from this large bill, and that was about to cripple us. Bart began to tell us that if we could not pay, he would lock up our doors in order to auction off our assets and freeze our checking accounts. It was then that I felt the Holy Spirit come upon me with a simple word: "Ask him about a payment arrangement." I asked if I could speak, and everyone kind of stopped and just looked at me.

I said, "How about a payment arrangement?"

Immediately the IRS agent responded with, "Okay, talk to your accountant and get back to me."

What a relief. But it was temporary, as now we had to come up with a plan that would satisfy the IRS. This burden was heavy. I felt like I was in a bubble with this catastrophic event all around me. My livelihood and income were at stake. I had four young children and Audrey to provide for. I felt fear and doubt hovering around me, but not infiltrating me, as I had peace in my heart. I know this bubble and peace were from the Lord.

Our accountant talked to Bart, and they came to an agreement. Due per week was $3,000 every Friday until the bill was paid. Otherwise, they would lock the doors and sell all the assets. This was a huge and difficult undertaking, but we had no other choice. Another word the Lord gave me prior to this was that my ministry would deal with impossible situations.

To be honest, this situation fits the bill as a trial, tribulation, and an impossible situation. I had to stay close to the Lord to keep my sanity. It was hard to believe the words he gave me prior to this, that he would get me through. I remember talking to Eddie before this surfaced. I knew it was only a matter of time before something like this would happen. My brothers and I would argue about it, looking for solutions. I had even thought about leaving the company the year before when I wasn't seeing eye to eye with my brothers. Eddie advised me to stay. So here we go. It's going to take God to get us out of this situation. We started the process by giving ourselves a pay cut.

This was particularly hard on me since I was raising a young family. Some weeks I was only taking home $200 a week. We would then make up the difference in the following weeks when the company could afford it. This went on for a while. We owed money, not only to the IRS but also to the state, the city, and our wholesalers. We were making changes within the company to help tighten our budget. I also started to go on jobs in addition to being in charge of the office. We tried everything. We tried to get loans from banks. We refinanced our own personal homes. We changed our accountant and refiled our tax returns. We made many of our employees subcontractors to help save on payroll taxes. I periodically would do a side job to help make ends meet. All in all, we were able to reduce our tax liability from $186,000 to $141,000. There was still a long way to go. Then something began to happen.

Keep in mind that I had been praying and seeking direction each and every day. It became evident to me that we had to live our lives one day at a time, trying to balance our payroll for all the employees. The amazing thing was that the word the Lord gave me, "How about a payment arrangement," seemed to work with everyone. Even many of our employees were willing to wait for a paycheck from time to time. Suddenly, I began to see God's hand in all of this. He was stretching out the timeline of all our creditors until we could get on our feet again. Also, sales suddenly were picking up. It's funny how God works sometimes.

At the church, Eddie had been teaching about Jesus always being in "the middle of the road." It was a theme. He had been focusing on how we, too, should model our lives after him, living "in the middle of the road." The reason I bring this up is to show how God gives us glimpses that he is with us. For example, during this hardship, I was helping my brother sell jobs.

One day, when I was in a customer's house bidding to replace their furnace, I gave the homeowner three furnace options. The customer responded with, "Give me 'the middle of the road' furnace." It was one of those moments when you are in the heat of the day in life and everything stops. God spoke to me through a stranger. The kicker to this story is that when I responded to him with the price, he immediately grabbed his checkbook and wrote out the check for the full job of $2500. That didn't just happen once. People kept writing checks without getting a contract first and would say, "Give me 'the middle of the road' furnace."

My brother, Dave, walked in one day and said a guy saw his truck and walked up to him. The guy told him that he was building a manufacturing plant and needed a heating contractor to install a system. He told my brother that if we could do it for $65,000 or less, the job was ours. It was a great feeling to see God's hand moving on our behalf. When your back is against the wall and there is no one else to turn to, God shows up. What a feeling! All my fear left that day. The scripture and his word to me became flesh. If God is for you, who can be against you?

I believed that if we were going to make it, I just had to hang in there, take it one day at a time, and allow God to steer us through the narrow straits of life. I was put in a position to trust God and only God. I got excited watching Jesus slay my problems. It felt so good being in the hands of God; I had such peace even though we were still in the midst of the problems. When Jesus showed up in amid my misery, it delivered me from all fear. It gave me comfort to be in a different place, a place of peace amid turmoil, uncertainty, strife, fears, and doubts. As it turns out, we were in the middle of having our biggest year ever. Thank God.

Well, you would think this is the end of the story. I felt like David in the Bible who kept escaping Saul. We were making the $3,000 a week payment, until one week, we did not have it. Yes, we were doing well but it was one of those times that no matter how well you planned or how hard you worked, you sometimes came up short. It was Thursday and the payment was due Friday. We had knocked the $186,000 IRS bill down to about $85,000 with penalties and interest over the past eight months. My desk was full of invoices and bills as I was trying to budget out the week.

When the phone rang, my secretary told me it was Bart from the IRS. What was I going to say? From the very beginning, Bart said if we can't make the payment, he would pull the plug and lock up the place. I didn't know what to say, but I picked up the phone anyway.

Bart replied, "Mike, I have only one thing to say to you."

I replied, "What's that?"

Bart replied, "Keep the faith," and hung up.

Tears filled my eyes. Once again, Jesus speaks to me through my enemy, the IRS, once again, I didn't know how God was going to do it, but I believed he would.

The next day, Friday, the payment was due, and once again, we didn't have it. We tried everything. People owed us money, but we were unable to collect it in time for today. At first, I thought, *Well, this is it, God never closes a door without opening a window.* I picked up the phone and called Bart; it was about three in the afternoon as we were waiting for the mail to come in hopes that a check or two would be in there to make this payment. It was the moment of truth. I believed God would get me through this, although it would be hard. Bart picked up the phone and told him that we did not have the payment.

Bart replied, "Well, we will let you skip this one." Can you believe it?

All the huffing and puffing with threats. Truly, God was in control and true to his word. In a year and a half, we made our final payment to the IRS. I was so happy. This unbearable weight has been lifted off our backs. I was so thankful to the Lord for getting us through this trial that I bought a ring to remind me of all that God did to get us through such a terrible storm of life. My faith and trust in the Lord had been stretched. It brought me to a new level of trust in him. Well, I would like to say that we learned our lesson and always did well from this point on.

The prior year and a half took a toll on many of our employees. We were unable to give them raises for their hard work, coming off our biggest year ever with most of the funds paying off debt. We birthed four new heating companies in the next year. My best friend, my brother-in-law, and my brother Tom's best friend decided to leave us and start their own company. At the same time, my brother decided to start his own company. All these men were our employees. Then our service manager decided to leave and start his own company.

Last, one of our mechanics took a job with one of our competitors as their installation manager. This all happened over the course of a year; we were left with a skeleton crew. We began trying to fill the gaps by hiring new employees. My brother's sons, who were apprentices at the time, were given crash courses to develop them into crew leaders. In the middle of all this, my father, Jerome, died in October 1994. What a tragic loss. He was eighty-four years old. I loved him dearly. I'm glad he got to see us pay off the IRS. He would call me every day to pick him up and bring him down to work with me. He would spend the day doing small but significant things to help us out and spend the day. He would come to our board meetings and give us support and encouragement through it all. His wisdom, good humor, and integrity were treasured by all. He would come to our prayer meetings from time to time. I will always miss him and my mother, who both laid such a solid foundation for me and my brothers and sister. It seemed that we got out of one fire, and were entering into another.

With all of this happening at the same time, this business was faltering once again. Unfortunately, we fell behind on all of our finances. This time it seemed different. The last battle took a toll on my brothers. The question was looming: can we get through this again? As things were worsening, my brother, Dave, decided to resign as vice president. We chose to file for a Chapter 11 bankruptcy, which allowed you to reorganize but still stay in business. This went on until it became obvious we were not digging out of it like last time. What was God saying with all of this trouble? It seemed like torture. After many discussions among ourselves, our attorneys, and our accountants, it was decided to file for chapter 7, "Liquidation bankruptcy." This was hard to believe for me. God had delivered me from a similar mess a couple of years back, but God wasn't done yet. It's true we filed for chapter 7, "Liquidation bankruptcy," but as I say, God always has the last word.

We took an inventory of all of our assets, inventory, trucks, and tools, all of which would be sold at an auction at the hands of a receivership operated by the bankruptcy court system. This was done at the same time that we decided to start a new company.

My brother, David, decided he was not going to be part of the new company. My brother, Gerald, and I decided we would put a new company in our son's name. Just as Jerome gave the business to us, we would give it to our sons. What we had was our customer base and our phone number, which produced about $1,200,000 in sales every year. It started with Gerald's two sons, who were already working in the business. Any of my children, who were younger, could join once they committed to working in the business. My brother, Gerald, and I would be employees and run the business until our children were able to do so.

As we were putting all this together, we were waiting for the courts to set a date for the auction of all of our assets. During this time, I was invited to a celebration at the William Westin Hotel with Eddie honoring Archie Dennis, the worldwide gospel singer. T. D. Jakes was the guest speaker. His message felt like it was aimed at me.

It was called "Operating in the Red." It fit what I was going through-serving God, constantly giving, living in the red zone.

"Believe your day is coming!" he said. God will not forget you, his word is the truth. And it will not come back void.

After waiting for about four weeks for the auction date to be set. I got inspiration from the Lord, which was, "Ask your attorney to see if you can bid on your old assets under your new company name." The new company name was Staab and Sons Inc. We had just started it. Our attorney called the receivership in the court system, and they said yes, we could make an offer. Wow! Praise the Lord. Losing all of those tools and trucks would have been detrimental.

All of our inventory totaled about $190,000, not including our buildings. The question was, How much we were going to offer? Well, under the circumstances, my brother and I had little to no money saved. So Gerard's two sons decided to apply for a loan. All they were able to secure was a $10,000 loan. Our attorney called the receivership at the court system and offered $10,000 on the $190,000 in assets that the receivership had. The receivership accepted it! So here we go; God once again came through. God truly has the last word! We escaped from the jaws of failure and were up and running like nothing had ever happened. The company prospered from that time on. It was still family-owned and operated in the fourth generation. I was able to retire after fifty years. Our sons are operating it now. There's only one catch: Being that we filed chapter 7 "bankruptcy" on the old company, Gerald and I were held personally liable for taxes of about $50,000. They were not asking for it yet, but it would be coming. It was one impossible situation after another.

Unfortunately, at the time, my wife Audrey was diagnosed with cancer of the bone marrow. They gave her three months to live. My children were so young: Elizabeth was nine, Matthew was fourteen, Kellie was sixteen and Sarah was eighteen. It was a traumatic time on top of everything else. It seems like my trials and tribulations were getting bigger and harder. How was I to tell the kids why was this happening to Audrey, who was only forty-one years old? I was fasting during Lent. My fast was getting up at 5:00 a.m. and praying for one hour.

After the diagnosis, Audrey remained in the hospital. At the time, I had no health insurance due to our financial dilemma at work. After this news, I went home and prayed, lamenting and asking the Lord what have we done wrong or why was this happening. The answer I got from the Lord was, "She's in my hands." That gave me some relief. That's the best place to be in a situation like this.

I remember going out to the community to talk to Eddie. I wanted to get his discernment of why this was happening. In the meantime, we had everyone praying for her. When I talked to Eddie, I asked him what the Lord showed him regarding what was happening to Audrey and our family. Eddie said he prayed to the Lord, and all he got was, "She is in His hands." This provided some comfort as it was the same word the Lord gave me. But next, they had to run Audrey's blood through a cleansing machine and were going to start her on intravenous chemotherapy once a week.

After a week in the hospital, we finally were able to get her home. We then were making frequent trips to the doctors regarding all the side effects, the chemo, and overall health management. It was looking bleak. Everyone was praying. Each time we went to the doctors, they would look at her blood to see how she was doing. The cancer of the bone marrow was preventing the reproduction of blood cells. It took about four weeks to get her strong enough to be able to go to a church service. We took her to a Sunday service.

As Audrey was coming up for communion, Eddie called her over because he wanted to pray for her. God has given Eddie a healing ministry. Once he finished praying for her, she got a very severe headache. It was so bad, we had to take her to a room inside the church to lie down. After a while, we took her home to rest. The next day, we went to the hospital for her weekly chemo treatment. Like every other visit, it started with taking a blood sample to see where her blood count was from the week before. We always had to wait for the results before they would start the next treatment.

When the doctor came in the first thing, he said was that there was a sensational change. Audrey had a normal blood count. The doctor proceeded to tell us that there was no medical explanation for this. It was impossible for the treatment to cause this normal blood count after chemo because your white blood cells are greatly reduced, causing you to be vulnerable to common colds and viruses. This was so out of the norm that the doctor was astonished. What did we want to do? Did we still want Audrey to keep getting the chemo treatment?

Audrey and I were both astonished as well. Did God heal her bone marrow at the Church service? We didn't know what to do. Was she cancer-free now? It was so hard to wrap our heads around it. We were not sure what was going on. We were thanking God, but wanted to be sure. It was too early to know if she was cancer-free for sure. On one hand, yes, we claimed it. On the other hand, was she truly completely healed? We were filled with such joy at the prospect that God had healed her. Audrey did not want to deny her healing but decided she was going to keep getting the treatment.

If God truly healed her, time would tell, so Audrey continued to get the treatments. When we came back a week later, there was no change in her blood count. It was still normal! The doctors were amazed that even her white cell count had not changed. That was so abnormal for chemo treatment because white blood cells always drop to almost nothing. When we came back the next week, it was the same thing.

The doctor looked at us as if to say, "If you don't believe you're healed, I sure do."

This was truly confirmation. There was no change after two more chemo treatments and no sign of any cancer! Hallelujah! Audrey was in God's hands. He healed her! The children, the family, the church, friends, and neighbors were ecstatic with joy. Audrey gave her testimony at the next church service.

At Audrey's last check-up, she wore a bumblebee broach that my mother gave her. When she checked into the office, the receptionist commented on the beauty of the broach and asked Audrey if she knew what it symbolized for a cancer patient. The receptionist said it symbolizes a cancer patient who has been healed because, scientifically, bumblebees can't fly. The wonderful thing about Audrey and my mom was how close they were.

The day Audrey was diagnosed was my mother's birthday and Audrey's last visit was the date my mother passed away years ago.

Strange, but true. Go figure. Well, another miracle! Thank God! Now I need another one to pay for the hospital and all of the doctor's bills. The hits just kept on coming. I felt like I had been through a war; battle after battle. I needed to trust the Lord, but it wasn't over yet. We had $225,000 in medical bills. It looked like I was totally in God's hands because I didn't have it.

Eddie's teachings on the cross and finding life through the cross of Jesus Christ had come to life in me. These crosses I had to bear propelled me into a deeper faith in a trust in God, which I don't think I could have done unless I was put into these situations with no other alternative than to trust God. It was the only way and I'm glad I did. For now, it has become flesh in my heart. No one can take away from me the reality that He is with us and that we can trust Him for everything. So it's time to pay the $225,000 in doctor's bills. It's funny how God works because many times when we can't come up with a solution ourselves, he brings one to us.

Of course, I prayed and prayed, thinking financially I was cooked for the rest of my life. This was just another heavy cross to bear, but Jesus is here! $225,000 is nothing for Jesus. I was preparing to do a service with a fellow minister, who had been laid off from his job but needed to provide for his family. He began sharing with us how tight his funds were and how his bills were piling up. I began to share with him how I had lost my healthcare insurance, and I, too, had numerous bills to pay.

He looked at me and said, "So what?" He said, "With my bills coming in the mail, I just throw them on the table and say, 'Here's another one for you, Lord.'"

At first, it sounded brash to throw that on the Lord. But I realized this man was a hard worker, not a slacker. If there was work to do, he would be doing it, because he hated being laid off. He, too, was in a tough situation. I'll never forget when he said, "So what?" I never felt guilty, nor did I measure myself against our society, which looks down on people who find themselves in difficult positions and can't afford health insurance.

Later that week, I got a call from a social worker from the hospital to talk about ways to pay the bills. She suggested applying to welfare and to a foundation called Hill-Burton. On the welfare side, I thought they would never give that to me. I recently owned two businesses and had a job with a steady income. I applied anyway. It wasn't too long after that that I got a call that they accepted my application. I applied to the Hill-Burton Foundation, and they also accepted my application. They didn't only pay all of our hospital and doctor bills, but now I had health insurance coverage for my whole family. Hallelujah! Hallelujah! God did it again. We were now almost completely out of the woods financially, but I still had one more hurdle to cross.

There was a $50,000 IRS bill attached to me personally because I was the secretary-treasurer of Jerome L. Staab & Sons Inc. When we filed chapter 7 "Bankruptcy," any tax debt left would go to the financial officers of the corporation personally. It was not too long after we settled the bankruptcy situation and started a new company under our sons' names that I got a letter from the IRS. This letter is from a different agent named Doug.

The office was in Washington, Pennsylvania, about a forty-five-minute drive away from Pittsburgh. We made an appointment. *Here we go again*, I thought. Only this time, I was on my own. I arrived, and I began talking with Doug, answering questions about my job. Somehow, we got on the subject that I was a minister. The conversation quickly switched to Doug, who was telling me about his divorce and how his ex-wife was taking him to the cleaners. He put his feet up on his desk to show me the bottoms of his shoes that had holes in them.

I started praying silently to the Lord for direction. Here I was, being interrogated on how I was to pay $50,000, and now he was showing me the holes in the bottom of his shoes. I wondered what was going on. I felt the Holy Spirit prompting me to ask him if he wanted me to pray with him. Doug quickly responded with yes, so we grabbed each other's hands. I led him in a prayer to ask Jesus Christ into his heart and forgive him for his sins. Doug began to weep. The weeping progressed more and more.

As joy filled Doug, the light of Christ was all over him. Well, I thought, this was a twist of events. I was spellbound observing God save the IRS agent in the middle of an interview with me over a $50,000 tax liability. What would happen next? After a couple of minutes of watching Doug weep his eyes out, he raises his head and asks me to please leave. He didn't want his coworkers to see him like this. I was getting up to leave, that he would fax me a very reasonable payment arrangement with instructions.

Of course, I agreed and got out of there pretty fast. I traveled back to the office and there it was: a $300 per month payment arrangement. I would pay the $300 per month for a year and then look into what is called an "offer compromise." I did as he said; I paid $300 per month. After a year, I applied for the offer of compromise. Basically, the IRS wanted to know everything I owned and what my net worth was. At that point, you can offer them your net worth which, in my case, was $5,000. I submitted all of the paperwork with the offer of $5,000.

At that time, I still owed the IRS about $48,500 with penalties and interest. Well, they accepted it. Thank God again and again for how he moves and covers us. Going through all these trials and tribulations made me think of when he called me to preach, that I would lead many through the trials and tribulations of life. What is this? Was he preparing me for something else?

CHAPTER

THE CHILDREN

Well, things were starting to smooth out to some degree. Audrey was doing well, cancer-free. Most of my debt was paid. During all this time, I managed to take my family on vacations to places like Emerald Isle in South Carolina, Disney World, Lake Erie, and mostly Pymatuning Lake. It wasn't always easy balancing my time with everything going on, but somehow, God would open doors for us to go camping at Hocking Hills, fishing, swimming, and taking pontoon boat rides at Pymatuning Lake.

Amusement parks like Kennywood were always an annual treat. I realized how much time I had been at church and work, so I always planned to do something with them besides the times we had at home. They were all growing up, and with that came trying to give them a good childhood and raising them in God's ways. Like any family, this presented its challenges. Part of raising them was a deal I made with them. A good report card and good behavior will grant them much liberty to do things like sleepovers, staying out later, visiting friends, and going to events.

On the other hand, if their behavior was poor or their report card was poor, then it would mean less liberty, and in more serious cases, grounding. Overall, they were very good kids, and I love them dearly. I used to make up stories at dinnertime to check how gullible they were and to teach them to not believe everything they heard. Some of the stories I would tell them would be things like, "Guess where I was today? I went golfing with President Clinton." Depending on their response to challenge my story, I would keep going until it became too obvious.

I always believed I had to prepare them for the world, to teach them the truth about life and what to expect in the world. I also taught them about choice, to know the truth about sex, drugs, and things like that. It was up to them to have the courage to make a good choice—to stand up for what was right and to not take any non-sense from anyone. Stand up for your friends and for those who are weak and cannot help themselves.

When my daughters got older, I would tell them how boys would try to take advantage of them to help them see the signs. I told them that if any of them got pregnant out of wedlock, they would not get a large wedding. Time went on. I would take Matthew, my son, out with me when we were building mission houses to learn the trade and hang out with the guys. We also took him to work at Staabs at a young age and had him help me fix stuff around the house. Over the years, they all helped or worked at Staabs at one time or another. I could never say enough about my wife, Audrey, and her influence on the children. She took the brunt of the burden most of the time. She and I would discuss our children every night when we went to bed or when we were alone. We always believed that both of us should be on the same page with how we were raising them.

Audrey would catch me up if I was out during the day at work or church. She mostly took care of the little problems, and I would take care of the big ones. Regardless of what problem or blessing it was, we always caught one another up at the end of the day. We would always receive great compliments on how well-behaved our children were. It was true. They were well-behaved for the most part. But going into teenage land, as we used to call it, we had our work cut out for us.

Our neighborhood in Arlington was a district on the south side of Pittsburgh, and it was violent. There were shootings, drugs, alcohol, sex, fights, and lawlessness. Trying to keep our children on the right path was job number one for both Audrey and me. Our biggest challenge came when they were getting older and going to high school.

Over the years, Audrey and I had many trips to the principal's office. Once we went to the juvenile court for Kellie and once to the Allegheny County jail for Matt, although all the issues were resolved and acquitted. Each of them wrecked my car at least once, three times it was totaled. Both Kellie and Elizabeth were in head-on collisions and walked away. God was protecting them over and over again. Matthew was falsely accused of an incident and was facing prison, but he was found not guilty. The same happened to Kellie in high school, as she was falsely accused, facing suspension, and was found not guilty. Sarah and Elizabeth primarily stayed out of trouble or maybe never got caught. They, like all teenagers, were pushing the limits, trying to experience life.

I found myself many times in protection mode because they all were beautiful young ladies and handsome men. The world was after them. There were times I had to chase down stalkers to threaten them and manage late-night phone calls from drunken classmates. Many times I had to depend on the holy spirit for direction when they would ask to sleep over someone's house or stay out after curfew. I always required them to go to church and children's and young adults' Bible schools as they got older. I would say a rosary every day for their protection had many adult conversations with them. We had such great times over the holidays and many times throughout the year. We both had big families and everyone would come over to our house for Christmas Eve.

Everyone took a turn at the holidays in our families. Kellie and Matt required the most discipline. I never thought they would give me a run for my money being I came from the streets myself, but they did. Thank God I had Jesus to help me. I used to tell them the reason they kept getting caught or busted was because their mother and I were praying for them. They were not bad kids, just wilder than Sarah and Elizabeth. I feel so bad grounding Kellie through most of her high school years, but I loved her so much, and I wanted to protect her. I always try to explain my disciplines to Kellie and

Matt. Matt got his taste of it as well. I would tell them that it was like they were ready to step out in front of a bus and get killed, and I would have to tackle them so they would not get killed because I loved them. If I did not love them, then I would let them do as they pleased. I was their father, and it was my duty to love them, which sometimes meant protecting them. They may not have understood it then, but I believe they understand it now.

On the other hand, with Sarah and Elizabeth, most of the time all I had to do was look at them a certain way and point them in the right direction. Of course, they were not perfect. No one is. They experience discipline as well. I know today that I owe all the credit to my Lord for helping me and my wife, Audrey, whom God used time and time again to raise them in love. Over the course of time, God gave them great husbands and wives, along with good jobs and many grandchildren and great-grandchildren. I always love my children, and God kept the deal I made years ago. I'll serve you, but you bless and keep my kids!

9

MISSION HOUSES

Over the past thirty-three years, I've helped build thirty-three mission houses for the Lord all over the country and the state. We had great fellowships in our church. We had people in every trade imaginable, from the architects to the carpenters to the electricians, to the painters, carpetmen, the decorators, to us, the heating, air-conditioning, and plumbing. The Community had grown very quickly. We made lifelong friends that we still keep in touch with today.

Once, I asked Audrey to go with me to Nashville, Tennessee, where we had a mission house run by one of our friends, Jim and Theresa. Audrey and I were taking them a stake bed truck full of furniture and supplies. It was a twelve-hour drive, and we had such a great time with Jim and Theresa. We were coming back home with another truckload of stuff from the mission house. Our truck was overflowing; we had to use a tarp to cover it and tie it down with rope. We left at five in the morning as I would need to be at work the next day.

Shortly after our departure, the tarp started to flap vigorously. We were going to need more rope. All of the stores were closed and we were on the interstate. I asked Audrey to pray with me for more rope and a place to find it soon. Otherwise, we would have had a mess with the tarp. Not even ten minutes after we prayed, a Jeep passed us on the highway and there was a large spool of rope bounc-ing off the highway where the Jeep was attached to its exhaust pipe.

I said, "Audrey, there's our rope. Let's follow that car." God has been so good to us. Who would think of rope on an interstate high-way at six in the morning? We were rejoicing and thanking the Lord, who made a way for us again. We made it home safe and sound.

There were many other things God did for us when we were building the mission houses. We were building a youth center in Conneautville, approximately 110 miles north of Pittsburgh. A few years prior, we built the mission house and the church on a property of about 140 acres. Two years before, when I was working at the church at that site, God spared my life. I was installing a water pump in a well that was recently drilled for the church. I had borrowed a drill from my brother, Ron, who lived in nearby Pymatuning Lake.

I brought my whole family with me, who stayed at a cottage my brother, Tom, owned in Pymatuning Lake. Tom left the business in Pittsburgh back in the early '80s and moved to Pymatuning and joined The Steamfitters Union. It was midmorning when I began drilling out the well casing of the well that would supply water for the church. I was in a four-foot-deep ditch, drilling a hole to fit the water lines that I would install into the well. While I was drilling, the drill shorted out. It was powered by 120 volts with an electric extension line from the church. The carpenters were framing the inside rooms of the church with compressor nail guns, making a lot of noise. No one was helping me outside.

When the drill shorted, it connected me to the drill and the well casing full of water. The shock froze me in a crouched position and I could not let go or fall away to disconnect myself from the shock that was racing through my body. I could not move, but I could yell. I started yelling, but no one heard me due to all the hammering going on inside the building. Seconds were flying by as I continued to yell for help. No one was coming. I began to fade consciousness as my life flashed before me. It was only a matter of seconds before I would be knocked out and no one would know.

After about forty-five seconds that seemed like a lifetime, Jimmy Dudash, a carpenter, must have heard me in between all the hammering. He came running out. At first, he thought something else was wrong until I was able to say, "Unplug me." He unplugged the extension line and I collapsed in the ditch, still conscious. I managed to crawl out of the ditch and lay flat in the grass beside the ditch. I felt like I was falling from a ten-story building. I was scared because I felt like I would have a heart attack. Many of my friends and brothers who were working inside came out to see what was going on. The church had a cemetery next to the church where I was working. Many of them started praying for me.

Then they started joking, saying, "Don't worry, Mike, if you die here, we will just carry you over to the graveyard and bury you! Ha, ha."

I didn't think it was so funny at the time, as my body was reacting to the electrocution. Finally, after about a half hour or so, I finally bottomed out. I felt like I had worked a twelve-hour day, and it was only morning. I was exhausted. I decided to take the rest of the day off. I went back to the cottage where Audrey and the kids were. Along the way, I stopped at a local bar and bought myself a six-pack of beer to take with me. I arrived at the cottage and told Audrey that I almost died that day. It had a great impact on me. I realized how quickly our lives could end. I gained a great appreciation for all of the little things in life and for my family. I drank a couple of beers with Audrey and enjoyed the precious gift of life that God spared me from losing that day. I am so thankful I've learned to appreciate each day and what it brings.

Two years later, it was time to build the youth house. It was 150 feet long, 50 feet wide, and 2 stories high. I was responsible for all the heating, air-conditioning, plumbing, two gas-powered generators, and two woodburners. It was a huge undertaking for one man to do on weekends. I originally told Eddie that I would need some skilled workers to complete it in a timely fashion. There were a few they could spare who had some experience in the field, but they were members from out-of-town mission houses. They would only be able to help one weekend a month, so I prayed to the Lord who sent me some help. Most were inexperienced in the field except for one, Tom P., who was helping me out in Pittsburgh.

I would be in Conneautville most weekends. It was difficult for Audrey and the kids for me to be away on weekends for most of the summer. I would bring my son, Matthew, with me on occasion. Tom P. managed to break away on Saturdays, which was a big help, along with other volunteers. I was amazed at how God used all these people. I wanted skilled people, but God had different ideas. I remember teaching one of the young adults named Jessie how to solder pipe one weekend. I guess I was a little desperate, myself. I laid out about 180 feet of pipe that had to be soldered or welded with a torch and put together. I gave him a crash course on a Sunday. Jessie was going to stay for the week to help me. I would be leaving later in the afternoon to go back to Pittsburgh. I left him with a prayer. I only imagined what I would find when I returned.

When I returned the following weekend, to my surprise, the whole 180 feet of pipe was soldered and put together with no leaks. Jessie was quite proud of himself. I was thankful to the Lord, who I believed guided him every step of the way. I know that was not an easy task for a beginner, and I give Jesse a lot of credit for having the faith to try. He was my apprentice, among others. They were all apprentices, except when the skilled labor from out-of-town mission houses showed up. Some would stay a week at a time, thank God. It was a lot of work.

What became evident to me was how God used unskilled labor through most of the project. It taught me an important lesson—to never deny the help God sends you. I was amazed to see God's hand move. I thought it could not be done without skilled help. God proved otherwise. God was putting this together. Unskilled people learn quickly after a few directions. I learned not to limit God in any situation; some of the many things God did during this project literally blew my mind at times.

As the building was taking shape, Eddie asked us to pray for beds. The second floor of the building would house fifty beds. During that time, there was a group of men who would travel in from Buffalo for our monthly miracle services. They heard about the need for beds. They knew of a university that was upgrading its dorms. We got all the used bed frames and dressers they were replacing, just like that.

They were oak dressers and metal frame beds in excellent condition. It so happened that at the same time, my neighbor in Pittsburgh stopped over at my house while I was in my garage. He asked me if I knew anyone who needed any mattresses. He worked at a university in Pittsburgh that was getting rid of all the mattresses and box springs in the dormitories. They were all in excellent condition.

We checked with Eddie, and he gave the green light to get them. Once again, all for free. God was moving quickly, putting this all together. One of the craziest things I experienced was when Eddie asked the church to pray for a safe to keep valuables. One day, I was picking up some supplies for the church in my stake bed truck at an Army and Navy store. I loaded the truck and was about to leave when this guy came running out of the store and flagged me down. I asked him what he wanted and asked me if I wanted a safe. I asked him what made him ask me that question. He replied that I was the first person he saw with a trunk big enough to haul it away. I asked him if it worked and said yes. I asked him how much he wanted for it. He said it was for free, as long as we hauled it out of there. This all happened within a week of Eddie asking everyone to pray. Miracles like this were happening left and right.

Eddie asked me to keep a lookout for a woodburning cooking stove. We came across two of them when we were looking for the wood burners. We found a coal company that had a used wood burner for only $200, which was a good deal. While I was talking with him, I asked him if he knew where I could find a wood-burning cooking stove. He said he had two used ones for $200 each. If we bought them brand new, they would be $1,200 each. I decided to go look at them, and they looked brand-new, so I bought all three for $600. What a deal. I never saw the Lord move so quickly as he did putting together this facility. That wasn't the end. We found two natural gas/propane generators along with two one thousand-gallon propane tanks for free as long as we purchased the propane from the people who sold us the tanks.

One day, the drywall guy, Mark H., was getting ready to hang drywall on the second-floor ceiling of the building we were working on. Hardly anyone showed up. I felt so bad for Mark. He was in a similar situation as myself. They were trying to figure out how they were going to hang all this drywall because it was heavy work. I could not see how the two laborers who showed up were going to do it alone. Then I heard someone coming up the steps. It was Jim O. who was six foot two. Tall Jim traveled all across the East Coast because of his job and I had not seen him in a while. He had traveled from New York to help, and here he was. Right on time. He decided to come in for the day to help. Well, that's all Mark needed. Jim could hold up the drywall while the rest screwed it into the ceiling. Each and every time, God has shown me He is not limited in anything. He will choose who he will choose to do his work.

Once, when I was locking up the doors in Pittsburgh at night, I came across two young boys who were crossing the street in the opposite direction as me. They were going one way, and me the other. I briefly looked at them; they were both about thirteen years old. Until now, I never had an incident over the twelve years of locking doors. God protected me and the people who lived at the church. There were shootings, stabbings, and robberies all around us every week, but it never touched me or anyone at the church.

Suddenly, as I made it to the other side of the street, one of the young boys called to me, saying, "Hey, mister, what are you looking at?" At first, I thought nothing of it as I turned to look at the two young boys. It appeared to me by the tone of his voice that he was trying to intimidate me. They were so young, and I responded with, "Why don't you go home to your mother?" Suddenly, one of them pulled out a gun and said to his buddy, "I should blow him away."

To my shock and surprise, I just stood still. It was one of those moments where you don't think; it's like you're frozen in a moment. Within moments, the young boy put his gun away and just shrugged as they continued on their way. It was obvious that God protected me.

Another time, as I was locking up, the Crips and the Bloods lived about two blocks apart with our church and houses in the middle. They were two violent gangs that roamed the streets of Homestead. I never had any problems with them until one night, when I was locking up, the Crips came running around the corner about two houses away from me in a shootout with the Bloods. I had to take cover between two parked cars as both gangs ran past me. No damage was done to the church or me. God, my Almighty in Jesus Christ with the Holy Spirit, protected me in the church again.

10

MARRIAGES AND DEATH

It was 1999. My oldest daughter, Sarah, was planning to get married. It was a joyful time for all of us. Audrey was healed now for a number of years, and we were planning our first wedding. The whole family was part of it. Sarah was twenty-three years old and met a good young man from the church, a wonderful man. He was also a minister named Adam. It was a fairly large wedding with over two hundred guests. I promised them a large wedding when they were young if they behaved themselves. Now it was time. The wedding service was at the church.

Audrey and I both had large families, and we were all excited about most of them coming to the church and being in the midst of the Holy Spirit. I remember talking with Audrey, Sarah, Adam, and the family to pray. The church was filled. It was a grand day to see everyone dressed up and walking my daughter down the aisle. The church was full and the service was blessed. They exchanged their vows, followed by a mass in communion. The music was blessed and the Holy Spirit fell on the congregation. The Lord began to move. There was great joy and jubilation. People were getting saved.

My sister, Vivian, began crying with joy, along with my niece's husband, Mike, who was also weeping with joy. So many more weeping with joy and even the videographer got saved. There was so much joy that filled the church. I remember going to the reception hall and observing my sister Vivian, Mike, and the videographer all still weeping with joy. It was an event remembered for a lifetime. Sarah and Adam bought a house not far from ours. It wasn't too long after in 2001 that our first grandchild was born, Olivia. She was a beautiful, healthy girl. We were now proud grandparents, talking and showing pictures to everyone. I remember being convicted and bragging about my grandchild as I used to criticize others when they went on and on about their grandchildren. Now I know why.

Kellie was next. I was so proud of her. She went through many rough times during high school. Some of the guys she was dating had me concerned. One night during the time she was dating, I came home to find her boyfriend crying in the corner of our porch. They were having some kind of disagreement. Kellie was standing about 8 feet away while he was crying. I looked at Kellie, and she looked at me with this expression of a part smile, and I can't believe this is happening look. Well, I left them alone and later talked with Kellie. He was a handsome boy, some kind of model. I had always hoped and prayed she would find the right person to marry. Someone who would protect her, provide for her, and love her. Ultimately, it would be her choice, of course.

Well, as time went on, God found her the right guy. After their turbulent teenage years, she found this guy named Dave. He was a car mechanic and a studio wrestler at night. At first, when she told me about him, I was taken aback. I visualize this big guy with tattoos all over his body. I remember meeting him for the first time. Kellie brought him home to meet us. When he walked through the front door, he was big, just about six foot two, and pretty well built. He was also very respectful when he first came over to shake my hand as we were introduced to each other. He only had one small tattoo, which was great. Last but not least, he was a Christian. Thank God.

Dave was the only one who had shown me respect. All the other guys were only after Kellie. This was a great sign and a great choice by my daughter. He was hardworking and big enough to protect her. He turned out to be a great guy with a big heart. I remember Kellie talking to me in her bedroom, deciding whether or not to marry him. I remember asking her if she loved him and if he loved her. I told her that their love for one another was the key to any marriage and to pray and ask the Lord to show her. Well, love conquers all. She decided to marry him. I was very proud of her.

Over the years, I have watched the Lord move on each of my children. Each one of them came to the Lord in their own way. They were all born again. I watched each of them make a turn in each of their lives from the world to God. I was so proud of each of them, choosing on their own to come to the Lord, with a little push from me and Audrey, of course, but God did it! That was the most important part for each of them in their lives. Audrey and I were truly blessed as each of them came to the Lord. We love them!

It was now 2001. I had been studying to become a priest since 1983. In 1990, I was ordained as a second diaconate, a step before becoming a priest. I was now preparing to be ordained a priest. The ordination was set for November 18. Audrey was at home, getting ready to come to the ordination. While she was getting ready, she noticed a large bumblebee flying around the room. It was a very strange event; bees do not normally fly around at this time of the year. I didn't know what to make of it. I remember the connection between my mother's bumblebee brooch and Audrey's last visit to the cancer center.

I often wondered if this was some kind of sign from my mother on the day of my ordination or maybe just a strange coincidence. Well, all went well at the ordination. I was now a priest. My whole family was there. It had been a long road and I was filled with joy and peace. Not too long after our ordination, I was celebrating mass with our bishop. There was a large crowd at the service of about five hundred people. We used multiple chalices to distribute communion.

As we were distributing communion, one of the priests, who was holding my chalice with the wine, noticed a miracle was happening. During communion, we would always dip the communion host into the wine and then distribute it to the person receiving it. The wine formed a waterfall all around the inside of the chalice and was recirculating and multiplying. This continued throughout the communion part of the service; we were all amazed. This wasn't the first time signs and wonders happened in the Community. We showed Eddie, our bishop. It was truly a solemn event. We saw many signs and wonders surrounding our masses.

Mostly, we witnessed answers to prayers that we would receive for others who asked us to pray for them. I started a prayer list as people asked me to pray for them. I would add their name to the list and lay it on the altar while I did mass. One woman had a son who was a drug addict. He dropped out of high school. She was torn. As we began to pray for them, she reported back to me. He started to come to the young adult ministry. Shortly after that, he joined the music ministry as he played the guitar. His life began to turn around. He stopped using drugs and was going back to get his high school diploma. She was so happy. He also expressed his love on Mother's Day to her with a loving card. She said she felt like she was walking on eggshells. Hoping this balloon would not burst. We kept praying for them as time went on and she reported back to me with more good news. He got his high school diploma. We thought by now, mission accomplished! Thanks to the Lord, but God was not done yet. He joined the church's chapter, the Third Order of Saint Francis. Later on, he got a job, met a Christian girl in the Community, and got married. What a change of events! Bless the Lord for answered prayers. Truly, God was moving in the ministry, and I give all the glory to Jesus. I know it was all him. He answered prayers.

Audrey had been healed for over seven years, but problems began to occur. I took her to the doctors, and they ran some tests. Apparently, the bone marrow cancer that she healed from seven years before had returned. Since the last time, medicine made advances in bone marrow transplants to treat this kind of cancer. Everyone was praying. My youngest daughter, Elizabeth, was now sixteen years old. We tried everything: bone marrow transplant, blood, transfusions, miracle services, chemo, and lots of prayers. Audrey was going through a lot of suffering. It was a constant back-and-forth, feeling fine one day and the next not. She began to get worse.

Audrey and I had a talk one day when she was in intensive care. She had a second bone marrow transplant the month before and she was not getting any better. At that point, she informed me that she was tired of being poked with needles. Being in the hospital over the past several months, her quality of life had diminished. She said that she was done with all of the procedures and was going to put her life in the hands of the Lord. She didn't want to live like this—always sick and going to the hospitals left and right. She said that God healed her once, and that if He wanted her to live, he could do it again. She wanted God to heal her so she could have a quality life. Otherwise, she wanted God to take her home.

The doctors tried everything. I realized that we were at another crossroads. I remember on the way home one day, I was talking with the Lord about the situation. He told me that he was going to take her home for a reason and a purpose. His words struck me to my core. It was now 2002, and Audrey was only forty-eight years old. I pleaded and asked the Lord if there was another way. Elizabeth was only sixteen. We kept praying, hoping the Lord would have mercy and answer our prayers for her to be healed and have a quality life. I decided to begin to prepare the children for the worst, but pray and hope for the best. I was so concerned for each of them.

I know what it's like to lose your mother. I talked to each of them privately. I explained that things were getting worse and that I wanted to prepare them in case the worst would happen. Each of them, in their own way, told me that they didn't want to see their mother suffer anymore. They wanted their mother to live a quality life, otherwise, they wanted the Lord to take her home. I was struck by their words. It was the same thing Audrey said. They were already prepared. Each one had the same response in their own words. I wasn't expecting this. God has already prepared them. I thought each of them would have difficulty accepting the notion she might die. I realized that this whole situation was in God's hands. It wasn't long after that Audrey came out of the hospital under hospice care. My cousin, Linda, was a hospice nurse who was going to take care of her. Audrey and Linda were close friends. We spent the following days doing what she wanted to do.

Meanwhile, everyone was still praying. Friends and family would visit Audrey. Audrey was still holding her own to some degree. She was able to venture out with help for short periods of time. Each of us had our own talks with her. Through all this time, I could not understand the Lord's word to me. A reason and a purpose, what on earth could that be? It was heart-wrenching to see my children deal with sorrow and to see Audrey suffering. What could be more important than a mother being with her children? I could not get my head around it, and I still can't to this day. Why? I decided to accept God's will with grief. It wasn't easy. I could've been mad at God, not understanding why he would let this happen.

Seeing the sadness of my children, I could understand why some people would not understand why a loving God would let this happen. It was a challenge to my faith and a crucifixion for me and my family. Will I accept my wife of twenty-eight years' death as God's will? Will I still love Him as much, watching my children experience this pain of death piercing our hearts? It's hard to accept. I guess everything I experienced prior to this in the trials of my life was only a taste of the cross. I've come to understand that crosses are things that happen that you have little to no control over. It's others that nail you to the cross; you can't nail yourself. Once in a while, you get a Simon to help you carry the cross. The cross is heavy, cold, and rough. The only way around the cross is to carry it. You can only do that if you face it and, out of love, you pick it up! You do it for others you love. You do it for yourself and if you love God, you do it for Him.

Audrey died. On the night of her death, all the children were sleeping over. They would take turns sleeping in her room to watch over her as she began slipping away. We all took turns giving her morphine at different times to give her some comfort. As I was sleeping in the room next to hers, I woke from a deep sleep at about 3:00 a.m. I decided to go in and check on Audrey. As I sat next to her, I began to notice her breathing was changing. I woke up the children and said, "I think it's time." We all gathered around her as each breath got further and further apart.

At 3:18 a.m., I'll never forget, she breathed her last breath. It was September 20, 2002. I had a great life with Audrey. Now she was with the Lord. The children cried as we all mourned. Her funeral was probably the largest the church had ever seen. People lined up for half of a block just to pay their respects. She was loved and respected by so many people. When we proceeded to the cemetery, we couldn't see the end of the cars that followed. I decided to do the burial service at the cemetery. She was buried next to my mother and dad.

As we began the burial service in her final committal, there were three bumblebees. Three of them circled the coffin as we sprinkled holy water and incense around her grave. There she was, being laid to rest next to my parents, and the bumblebees that kept circling around her. To me, they exemplified the love Audrey and my mother had for each other and this life journey that was now coming to a close but carried on in the heavens, but she's alive in another place, waiting and praying for the rest of us. We will see her again, without any suffering. In the days to follow, Sarah and Kellie would be going back to their homes with their husbands. Elizabeth and Matt were still home with me. I was deeply concerned for all of them as they were trying to adjust to a new life without their mother. We tried to get together often. It just wasn't the same without her. It was tough, to say the least.

A month later, I decided to take them all on a train ride up to Oil City, Pennsylvania. We needed each other. We had to stay close and stick together to try to patch this hole in our lives. I watch all of them mourn in their own way. I was very proud of all of them. I think I was so caught up with how each of them was handling this and if they were going to be alright.

I wasn't thinking about myself. It was very difficult. We received a lot of support from family, friends, and the church. I was thankful for that. Elizabeth was seventeen, a senior in high school. Matt was twenty-two and moved into his own apartment. Kellie was twenty-four, and Sarah was twenty-six, both married. Elizabeth was planning to go to college. Matthew was working at Staab & Sons Inc. with me. It's difficult to say how the death of a loved one can affect you. I want all my children to become strong adults who still love the Lord. It's not easy getting over such a loss and adjusting to it.

I remember talking to each of them, saying, "Life has changed as we knew it. We will have to adjust to the change." It's hard to change when you love your wife and the life you had with her. I guess that's what the cross is all about—change. It is easy to say, but very hard to do. You need God's grace, his love, and the help of others to do it. Otherwise, you'll fall under the burden of it. Each of my children was finding their way in all of this, and I had to find mine. Audrey's death left such a hole in my life. It wasn't easy to adjust to the change. Elizabeth helped me a lot, being she was still living at home. We leaned on each other a lot. We all helped each other. Matt was living with his cousin. Of course, Kellie and Sarah had their husbands and started their own families. I think it's when you're all alone that's the hardest. Elizabeth did a lot for me like shopping and cleaning, so I think it hit me the most when Elizabeth decided to go away to college.

Up until this time, all my attention was on my children, making sure they were okay. When Elizabeth announced that she was going away to college, it hit me all at once like a ton of bricks. Until now, I was always trying to remain strong for my family during this time of mourning. I was leaning on God, Elizabeth, and the rest of my children. We grew much closer during these times as we leaned on one another.

Months passed, and they were doing okay, but I certainly was not. I started to cry uncontrollably as we sat at our kitchen table. It seems like I have buried my emotions making sure everyone was okay. I couldn't stop crying, which is not like me. I went out on the deck, and Elizabeth followed. We decided to get out of the house and go for a drive. Elizabeth and I went to Mount Washington, which overlooked the city, still crying. We then went down to the park by the Monongahela River, still crying. We decided to get some ice cream. I finally got a lot out of my system, and we made it back home in one piece. Elizabeth was very comforting and understanding.

Here I was, trying to be strong for her, and she was comforting me. I still struggled. Elizabeth left for college, and I was home all alone. I remember going food shopping for the first time in twenty-eight years. Audrey always did it. I was lost. I remember calling out to her in the supermarket, praying to her to help me find stuff. Between food shopping, clothes washing, and many other things, I had to adjust. Elizabeth would come home on weekends sometimes.

Sarah and Kellie jumped in from time to time to help me. I was finally making a change to live alone.

As time went on, my daughter, Sarah, and her husband were moving to California. The Community had a mission house there. Adam is going to assist a pastor as his assistant. It was a big step. It put more of a burden on Kellie, who invited me over for dinner a lot. She adopted some of our family's traditions in gatherings like Christmas Eve. Kellie did a lot in the days to follow, with Sarah living in California and Elizabeth away at college, to organize the family get-togethers. She organized the family visit to Sarah in California for a shower, among others. As time moved on, Matthew was in plumbing school and working in a new plumbing department I started at Staab & Sons Inc. Elizabeth was transferring to a college in Pittsburgh after two years of being away. She would now move back home with me.

In 2004, Kellie and Sarah gave birth to two more grandsons, Kyle and Jordan. God was patching up our lives. In 2005, Matthew met a Christian girl in the Community named Brooke, a beautiful young lady. She really helped fill the gap in his life. It wasn't too long after in 2007 that they decided to get married. It was another beautiful wedding. Between Elizabeth coming back home, Sarah and Adam moving back to Pittsburgh, Kellie and Sarah birthing two more grandchildren, and Matthew now planning his wedding, the sorrow that had consumed our hearts was now met with joy. The word of God says that the joy of the Lord is our strength. God was strengthening our family. The sorrow was easing away and the joy was growing. You never really forget the sorrow, but the joy makes it tolerable.

CHAPTER

11

A NEW LIFE

In 2008, one late September Sunday afternoon, Jim asked me as he was walking out of our church if we would baptize his forty-year-old daughter who was going through some troublesome times. We had an Immersion service scheduled later that week on a Thursday night, at 8:00 p.m.

Bonnie showed up that night—beautiful and attractive. Kind of like the one I've been praying for the last couple of years since my late wife, Audrey died almost six years before.

My daughter, Elizabeth, was engaged to be married—the last of my three daughters and one son. And now that she was on her way, finishing college and all, I thought it was an appropriate time to start looking for love again.

I fell in love once with my first wife, Audrey, whom I met in seventh grade. We were high school sweethearts and married at twenty-one. Four children later and now 14 grandchildren later, with one on the way. Audrey died in September of 2002. Now it's 2008. Liz and I, along with my other three children, pulled each other through a very difficult time. When you love somebody, time goes very slow when you lose them. It took time for all of us to get on our feet. I felt I was the last. I felt I had devoted much of my time to making sure I stayed strong and that my kids were alright. Now Liz was ready to fly the nest. That's where my life with Bonnie begins.

This was not a slam dunker. Bonnie, a beautiful lady who owned her own business, had some problems that she was going through. I was a preacher of the Gospel at night and on Sundays, and a heating and air-conditioning contractor by day. Nevertheless, this was the day the Lord had made when he brought Bonnie into my life for the first time.

It was a Thursday night, and we were having an Immersion service along with a prayer meeting, something we regularly do every Thursday night. As assistant pastor of the Community of the Crucified One, this was one of my assignments: to have prayer meetings every week and Immersion services as needed. Bonnie really needed to get baptized—she was a single mom, divorced with three children, and now several years later broke up from a recent one-and-a-half-year relationship.

With the youngest child at nine years old, the middle at fifteen, and the oldest at seventeen, she had her hands full. I didn't know any of this at the time, but God did.

Bonnie came from a Christian background. She found a relationship with God through her aunt at the early age of ten years old. Later, she met her first husband in high school and got married young. Her husband then left her, and they got divorced. She was a single mother, left to cope with three children and a business. This began the difficulties for Bonnie.

All the pressures of life led her to a life of providing for herself and her children, and at the same time, trying to get her life back together. Dating, break-ups, friends, drama, hoping for the right guy, balancing her life with her kids, her job, and her family round and round, sometimes up, many times down. Disappointment after disappointment. Never settled. It seemed like everything was falling apart for her. She was now forty, and I was fifty-four. You would think age would make a difference in this relationship. Well, it did at first.

Bonnie got baptized that Thursday night in the fall of 2008. She became a regular at the Thursday night prayer meetings that we held. After the prayer meeting one night, Bonnie asked me if she could take counsel with me. Up until now, I've seen many attractive women come and go. None truly interested me on a personal level—well, maybe a little bit. But none really attracted me to the level that I would like to get to know them personally. There were a few women along the line that became interested in me. I mean, I never had any problems getting women in my younger days before preaching the Gospel, so it seemed I still held some attraction, but I had not met anyone since Audrey's death that attracted me to the point that I wanted to begin a relationship with them. Something was always missing.

This was the first time that Bonnie and I ever talked one-on-one, privately and personally. She began to tell me about her personal life and many personal things. As a minister, my first duty is to help the individual with their spiritual, mental, or physical needs—whether it be counseling, praying, coaching, encouraging, or guiding. As I listened intently to her conversation, I began to see a quality in this woman that I had not seen, except in those who for one reason or another were unavailable. This woman was sincere, caring, honest, smart, well-kept, and most of all you could tell that she loved. It was the love that I had not seen in all the other women, not like I had seen in her.

That created a spark within me. I had always known my first duty was to the Lord and to help this young woman get through all her problems, and she had many, but now the personal side of me became very interested in Bonnie for a lot of reasons.

12

A SIGN

I have to go back now to give you a true perspective of what just happened. When Audrey died eight years before, I purposed within myself that I would not bring another woman into my house while my youngest daughter, Liz, was still in high school or college because I did not want to hurt her or confuse her. I purposed myself that not until she and the rest of my children were on their feet would I only consider engaging in another relationship. So up to now, I wasn't really looking, knowing I would not permit myself that pleasure at the cost of my daughter's well-being.

Now Liz was graduating from college and getting engaged. I had prayed to the Lord back in 2005 regarding my future in reference to this, as to whether or not He wanted me to marry again—whether He would want me to have a companion, or to be alone with Him for the rest of my life. He answered me with these words: *I would get married again. He would bring her to me at the right time, and she would be infatuated with me.*

The sign I would be looking for was that *she would be infatuated with me.* The rest remained to be seen.

Well, the conversation with Bonnie became quite lengthy that night. Everyone had left, and it was just the two of us sitting on the back patio with nothing except the soft sounds of the night, the heavens above, and our conversation.

I counseled her, without going into too much detail for personal reasons. I advised her to get back to being close to the Lord and to change some of her practices. She responded by stating the difficulties of implementing these changes on a consistent basis. I responded that if she found herself in a tight spot, she could call me, and so I gave her my number.

It wasn't too long after our first counseling that Bonnie consistently fellowshipped at the Thursday night prayer meetings.

She went out of town during Thanksgiving to visit family in Detroit. I was working late at my job on Sunday when she called on her way back to Pittsburgh to talk.

I suggested we meet at the Olive Garden for dinner, as I had not eaten yet. She agreed.

We met at the restaurant and ate a fine dinner, where we talked and talked some more until the restaurant was ready to close. We were the last couple in the quiet dining room.

Much of our conversation was me ministering to Bonnie about her difficulties, mixed with swapping stories about each of our lives. We were getting to know one another better. Time flew by so quickly, just like the other night after the prayer meeting. I could not remember the last time I closed a restaurant or the last time I talked to a woman for so long. Little did I realize that when it came to talking with Bonnie, things were only getting started. Normally, my conversations in and outside of ministry only lasted ten to fifteen minutes—get to the point, offer the remedy, and I was finished. So it seemed strange to me that I could talk for so long with her.

During our conversation at the restaurant, I invited her to call me any time she had a question. It was not long after that she called me again. We talked on the phone for nearly three hours. That last phone call was filled with talk about the Lord, the Bible, and Bonnie's newly resurrected faith that she had in Jesus. It seemed she had this thirst to learn and know more about the Lord.

The problems Bonnie was facing in life seemed to be the basis of these lengthy conversations. Some nights we talked for two hours—

other nights two and a half. One night's discussion lasted nearly four hours. This was all new to me because I never talked on the phone with anybody prior to this for more than fifteen minutes. Each conversation seemed to take us deeper into each other's lives—sharing about the Lord, the Bible, our families, our problems and experiences, and the many things I had seen God do in my own and other people's lives over the years of ministry.

The phone calls started with once a week, then in time to twice a week. Normally, this would have been an aggravation for me, but not with Bonnie. It seemed like we would start talking and just get lost in this vacuum of timeless and endless conversation. Whether we were laughing or serious, every talk had this sense of timelessness.

I used to think, *How on earth do we find so much to talk about?* But it seems that when the Lord is in the midst of it, it could go on forever, and it feels like it has.

Some days, the conversations would be shorter, but that's only because they became more frequent. Even though we started talking almost every day, there was always one or two long conversations. It seemed inescapable with Bonnie, but I really liked it.

In our conversations about the Lord and everything else, it seemed Bonnie was hitting a wall in her personal life. In those days, the Lord began to expose aspects of her life that she knew needed to be changed. One such aspect was the company she kept. The more Bonnie wanted to change her life, the more her friends would try to pull her back.

One day, after a revelation of this, she decided to cut ties with this old culture of friends and focus on a new culture of living with respect to a Godly way of life. This path presented challenges for Bonnie. Stepping away from the old culture of friends and developing new ones—this is where I came in. I expressed that if she ever found herself alone, with nowhere to go, she could call on me.

I began to notice a sincere effort from Bonnie in this regard. It was then I proposed for her to come with me to some Christian gatherings, such as birthday parties and other Christian services. This would give Bonnie the opportunity to meet other Christians, which could hopefully help her new walk with the Lord. One party that we attended was a fiftieth birthday party for my original pastor's wife. Many people were invited and I thought this would be a good way for her to meet new people.

I remember picking Bonnie up at her house in Baldwin. This would be the first time I picked her up for any event. I told her that it would be good for me also, in that I was always used to going to these events alone for the last six years. It was really nice for me to have some companionship and I believe it helped Bonnie make the transition. I thought we had a wonderful time together. The party boasted a DJ, and I was able to introduce Bonnie to some of my long-time friends. Bonnie seemed comfortable—she danced, the food was amazing and so was the fellowship. We stayed fairly late before the time came to take her home.

We talked the whole way home, and I realized I really liked Bonnie. I admired her courage to step out in faith and put forth this sincere effort to follow God's will for her life.

I began to develop feelings for Bonnie. I truly enjoyed talking with her, and now I enjoy being with her.

Near the end of that drive home, I told Bonnie how much I enjoyed spending the night with her. I went a step further and spoke up: "I would like to see more of you."

Bonnie was quiet for a moment, then responded, "I think you need someone more mature."

I followed up by saying I was fine to move forward, but I realized she wasn't. Anyone who knows me knows that I don't give up quickly. I decided not to push the issue at the moment. After all, everyone is entitled to their choices, and I felt I was entitled to mine. Maybe it was too soon. I decided to give it some more time to develop and see which way it would go. With that said, I felt good expressing my feelings to her. I dropped her off at her house and called it a day—a good day.

After this, we went through a period of going out to dinner, as *friends*, of course. Bonnie made that perfectly clear, week after week, month after month. It wasn't that I kept pushing her to be more than friends, it was simply that I enjoyed her company and knew she enjoyed mine. She kept calling me on a regular basis, and we were going out to dinner weekly. It felt like everything was firing on all cylinders, except for the fact that Bonnie claimed she couldn't see herself in a relationship with me. This was very hard for me to understand. How can you get along with someone mentally and spiritually, but not emotionally? This is where things really get complicated. I had no idea why we could not get past just being friends. I had desired to kiss her, but she would not let me. Then we would talk for an hour as to why we were "just friends." I would contemplate, *Maybe it's my age or my appearance*. I'm fourteen years older. Perhaps some, or all of that was true, but she would never say specifically why.

One night we went out to dinner. It was a snowy, freezing rain type of night with very little traffic due to the weather. We basically had the whole restaurant to ourselves when suddenly, this older gentleman came in from the bar, saying, "Take it slow."

It hit me like a ton of bricks. I knew this was meant for me to take it slow with Bonnie. How slow, I had no idea. This would befuddle me, as we seemed to be a perfect match, compatible in so many ways. We never really had a serious argument to speak of, and it's been over a year of long phone calls, coming to every service, counseling, dinner, and watching television together. Bonnie inviting me to her family functions, and me inviting her to mine was what seemed to be missing. God only knows. Then something strange happened.

By now, my daughter, Elizabeth, was set to be married. She was also working for Bonnie at her daycare business, and my other two daughters were using her daycare for my grandchildren. It was during this time that I asked Bonnie if she would be my escort at Elizabeth's wedding, as I didn't want to have to go through all of the festivities alone.

She agreed.

During the time up to my daughter's wedding, things were going fine, but now they seemed to start to fall apart.

Out of the blue, Bonnie told me that she met someone on a Christian dating service online, and now that she was dating this guy, she didn't want things to get funny between us as she still valued our *friendship*. But we really could not be going out to dinner, and other things of that sort.

This was devastating to me. Just when I thought we only had one more hurdle to cross, and I would have a newfound wife whom I loved. Maybe I didn't see the handwriting on the wall. Maybe I was living in this denial of just being *friends*. Maybe Bonnie meant what she said a year and a half before. Anyway, I asked Bonnie about the wedding (being my escort), and she said that she would still do it.

My daughter's wedding was great. It was wonderful having Bonnie by my side. Some things just seem "so right." But anyway, this is life. Sometimes, you can't always get what you want, but was this the case? Maybe just a bump in the road? Who knows.

I began to pray. It was funny because, even though Bonnie was dating this guy, she would still call me. Not as frequent and not as long, but she would still call. She still came to the church services and prayer meetings. She still took counsel with me. I didn't understand at times because she would discuss certain domestic issues that arose with her family—issues one would normally discuss with a boyfriend. It seemed our compatibility never ceased. However, one night Bonnie's dad asked me to talk to Bonnie about an incident involving her son. We didn't see eye-to-eye that night, as we had our first serious argument involving her family.

We ended up on opposite sides of the fence that night, and she didn't show up for prayer meetings for two weeks. She was upset. I used to wonder how she balanced this relationship in her life. Maybe it was truly falling apart. I continued praying about all this, the "bump in the road" and all. I know I loved her, and I believe that she loved me too. Even though she had been seeing this guy for a year now, this mystery began to confound me. It drove me deep into my prayer closet, for why was this happening? Was this the way it was supposed to be—just friends? Why was this boyfriend still in the picture? Was I just stringing myself along with a false hope that things were going to change?

So I went to the Lord with a *fleece*. I asked the Lord to show me beyond a shadow of a doubt if I was to continue to entertain this whole situation with Bonnie and wait for her to come to her senses, or me to come to mine. I prayed and said to the Lord that I was tired of my emotions rolling back and forth about this woman, that I needed a sign as to whether I should still carry the hope of being together, or get over it and move on. At this point, I gave the Lord one week to continue this lopsided relationship with Bonnie. Otherwise, I would wean away and accept the fact that we are truly just friends, and not engage in conversation as much as we had.

It was June now, 2010. Two years transpired, and it was time to put this to the test. One week.

Three days later, all my children and grandchildren were going to Kennywood, our local amusement park in Pittsburgh. They invited me to come and spend the day at the park. I had just prayed two days prior for a sign from God if I was to continue in this closer-than-normal relationship with Bonnie. I had parked my car in the upper lot and thought I would take the lift into the amusement park. As I cruised down into Kennywood, I had been contemplating my prayer regarding Bonnie. I figured I would walk through the park and look for my family.

Shortly after entering, I saw Bonnie with her sister, Kathy. They saw me at the same time, and we greeted one another by the bridge near the merry-go-round. *What kind of sign was this? Bridge? Merry-go-round?*

Immediately, Kathy took control of the conversation and said that she was leaving. Bonnie was going to be there by herself while her son, Alex, was riding rides with friends. Kathy asked me if Bonnie could walk with us. I felt obliged and asked Bonnie if she'd like to come with me and my family around the park. She accepted the offer. The next thing I knew, we were walking through the park together, and again it seemed so right. *What was happening to me?* She is dating someone else, and here we are walking through Kennywood together.

It began to rain, and we found shelter at the restaurant where we had dinner with my family. The rain ceased as we exited the restaurant, and the sky above burst with the most beautiful rainbow. Bonnie held my youngest granddaughter, Elyse, as we walked through the park. The rest of the night was full of bright lights, swirling rides, and conversation, and again it seemed so right.

The night wore on, and my family departed for home. As they left, Bonnie and I were seated in a park. We resolved our previous argument regarding her family through a long discussion. We concluded the night by praying with each other as the park closed up, and it seemed *so right*.

Well, I had asked God for a sign, but she's with another guy. A younger guy than me and well-off with a business. What was to become of this?

13

DEALING WITH
MY EMOTIONS

I've been preaching for twenty-nine years. I assisted my bishop for twenty-one years. My bishop recently died, and the new bishop asked me to be his assistant pastor. I've served him for two years at this point—it's 2011, and I'm now fifty-six years old. Things are changing rapidly. All of my four children are married and have their own children. Fourteen in all. The church I belong to is moving slowly in a different direction, and God started to deal with me in a whole new way. I've also been part of the eldership in our church. The new bishop I've known since he was a child (now a good man) is one I've always liked. But I felt God moving on me to leave the church I have served since 1978, thirty-three years, and start a new church called Way of New Life Ministries. I left my old church with grace and blessing. Although it's always difficult to leave old friends of thirty-three years, the pressing of the Holy Spirit in my life to begin this new church was undeniable. With several confirmations of this shift in a two-week period, I knew I must follow the Lord.

Follow Him I did, and Way of New Life Ministries officially opened. My life was truly entering something completely new.

Bonnie is one of the church elders, and I am the pastor. This relationship took a dramatic turn in 2011. Bonnie got engaged to

85

be married to the man she had been dating. What a blow. She didn't even tell me about it. I heard about it through the grapevine at our church. She tried to avoid the topic with me altogether.

At this point, I had some burning questions for the Lord:

1. Why bring this woman into my life, who is seemingly enthralled with me, that You said would be a sign for me to look for?
2. Why, after attempting to part ways with Bonnie, would you give me the strong sign I believed to have received on that special day at Kennywood?
3. What's going on?

The Lord answered me with these words: "The relationship would not last." This referred to Bonnie's relationship with her fiance.

My reply was, "The relationship won't last?" I couldn't understand why there was even a relationship, to begin with! Surely, this was going to take every bit of faith I had. Why not just dump her and move on? But I loved her. Yes, this seems ridiculous. Why does it have to be so complicated?

After my whole discourse of venting my frustrations, I always depended on the Lord's Word in my life. At this point, waiting to watch this whole scenario play out was not going to be easy. Actually, it felt impossible. One of the truths the Lord had brought to me early in my ministry was that the Lord would charge with me "impossible situations." He prepared me to deal with impossible situations by taking me through them in my own life.

One example of this came when our heating company had to file Chapter 11 Bankruptcy, followed by chapter 7 "Bankruptcy." I was secretary-treasurer at the time, and we owed the Internal Revenue Service $186,000.

To make a long story short, we paid off the IRS and the city within a year and a half. We got all of our $190,000 worth of assets back for $10,000. I've been through many traumatic situations. People pulling guns on me; head-on car crashes; death of close loved ones; children getting into trouble with the law and car crashes of their own, totaling three of my vehicles—just to name a few of those situations.

Throughout my life, I feel like I've lived the song that says, "I've seen fire, and I've seen rain." Simultaneously, though, another song sang in my heart with the words, "I've learned to trust in Jesus, I've learned to trust in God." One thing God taught me in life was to never give up unless God says so!

God has always come through for me. Through the thick and thin, truly I have "learned to trust in Jesus, I've learned to trust in God." I've learned not to lean on my own understanding, just like in the case of Bonnie's engagement. Whom do I trust? Do I trust what appears to be the end of my hopes with Bonnie? Or do I trust God in the face of disaster? On that day, I found out the wedding date had been set.

One thing I will add to this point—without going into too much detail—is that God sent me small signs regarding this situation all along the way. The signs came usually when I was ready to call it quits. One sign was that Bonnie did not invite me to her wedding. However, she called me on her way to the wedding unknowingly. All I could hear was the bridal party carrying on—strange, right? After a year of marriage, they were talking about divorce, and then they got divorced.

It wasn't easy living through this period, but as I said earlier, God had prepared me to face these impossible situations. Another aspect of my calling, when God first called me to preach, was that I would "lead many through the trials and tribulations of life."

Now here was Bonnie going through a divorce.

I decided I would not chase Bonnie. I believed that if it was truly from God, he would bring her to me at the proper time as He promised. It had to be right in order for it to work.

Anyone who knows me knows that I'm a realist. I was not going to chase her and have it end up being a one-sided love story or something phony, so I decided to just leave it in God's hands and see what the Lord would do.

Time went on. It was a rough road for Bonnie going through all of the divorce proceedings. But then it was all over. She continued coming to the prayer meetings and other services we held at Way of New Life.

Then one day, Bonnie called. She wanted to come over and talk with me. I told her that was fine; I figured it was about something she was going through, or who knows what. It could be anything.

It was early in the evening when Bonnie came over to the house. She came in quietly, pretty much like herself. She sat on the couch, and I was seated in a chair across the room from her.

Keep in mind that at no time during this period did I ever insinuate the idea of us seeing each other. I really didn't know what to expect. Bonnie could bring up matters involving the church, her work, and her family—it could be just about anything, and then she said it.

Bonnie said she wanted to talk about the love we had for each other but never discussed it. I was floored. Bonnie was saying that she loved me.

It was the final hurdle after all these years of wondering what was wrong because we seemed to get along so well. The whole "just friends" thing, the "more mature woman" thing, the "boyfriend" thing, the "engagement" thing, the "wedding" thing, the "divorce" thing…now it was "my" thing.

I rose up off the chair, walked across the room, and kissed her for the first time, and then I kissed her again. Suddenly, we were on the same page. God had shown me the faithfulness of his word. Bonnie and I got married seven months later.

Don't ever give up on God's word no matter what it looks like. Sometimes we must go through tests of our faith. Sometimes, people's choices get in the way.

I've learned to trust in Jesus!

I've learned to trust in God!

14

WHAT'S NEXT?

It's 2022. Bonnie and I have been married for seven years. Our children, Bonnie's three and my four, have produced a total of twenty-one grandchildren and three great-grandchildren, twenty-four and all. Both of Bonnie's sons, Alex and David, have good jobs. Caitlin, her daughter, married a Christian man several years ago. My four children, Sarah, Kelly, Matt, and Liz, are all married to Christian spouses. All have Christian children with good jobs, and everyone is doing great.

Also, our church, Way of New Life Ministries, is doing great as well after eleven years. I want to thank God for all of His blessings. Bonnie has been at my side since the beginning of Way of New Life. Her support has been unwavering. I know God has put us together in ministry. She runs the children's ministry and is still an elder of the church. Our discussions on matters in the church help keep me grounded and are of great value to me, especially her discernment.

When I look back, God spoke to me about "leading many through the trials and tribulations of life." I wonder sometimes if what I went through over the past forty-seven years was preparing me for what might be coming on the face of this earth. God has been speaking to us at the church and all who will listen to get close to Him. Not to look to governments or institutions but to look to Him as He will guide them through what is about to happen on the earth. He will protect them, provide for them, and be with them. God only knows what's coming. If you're reading this, get close to Jesus. Follow Him and His Holy Spirit. He will not let you down.

ABOUT THE AUTHOR

Pastor Michael R. Staab is currently the pastor of Way of New Life Ministries which he started in 2011. He was born in Pittsburgh, Pennsylvania, in 1954. He has four brothers and one sister. He was married to Audrey Schank in 1975 after they had both accepted Christ as their Lord and Savior. They had four children together. He was called to preach the Gospel in 1978 while running a heating and air-conditioning company with his three brothers. He was ordained to preach the gospel in 1983 after attending seminary for five years at the Community of the Crucified One, a nondenominational Christian church where they were members. He then served as an assistant pastor to his bishop from 1987 through 2011. The Lord then called him to start a new church called Way of New Life Ministries, a nondenominational Christian church.

His first wife, Audrey, passed away in 2002. He has seventeen grandchildren and three great-grandchildren. He remarried Bonnie Martinez in 2015, who had three children of her own and four grandchildren. He retired from the heating and air-conditioning company in 2022. He and his wife, Bonnie, now enjoy the full-time ministry at their church Way of New Life Ministries. You can find their ministry on the web at wayofnewlifeministries.org or on YouTube at Pittsburgh Preacher Man, where they post all their Sunday service messages.